Helga Fritzsche

Cats

Everything about Acquisition,
Care, Nutrition, and Diseases

With 26 Color Photographs by Outstanding
Cat Photographers
and 55 Drawings by Fritz W. Köhler

Translated by Helgard Niewisch, D.V.M.

Woodbury, New York • London • Toronto • Sydney

First English language edition published in 1982
by Barron's Educational Series, Inc.
© 1978 by Gräfe and Unzer GmbH, Munich,
West Germany

The title of the German edition is *Katzen*.

All inquiries should be addressed to:
Barron's Educational Series, Inc.
113 Crossways Park Drive
Woodbury, New York 11797

Library of Congress Catalog Card No. 81-19073
International Standard Book No. 0-8120-2421-4

Library of Congress Cataloging in Publication
Data
Fritzsche, Helga.
  Cats: everything about acquisition, care,
nutrition, and diseases.
  Translation of: Katzen.
  Bibliography: p. 75
  Includes index.
  1. Cats. I. Title
SF442.F7413   636.8   81-19073
ISBN 0-8120-2421-4   AACR2

PRINTED IN HONG KONG

45   490   98765

Inside front cover: Siamese cat with kitten
Inside back cover: Two house cats
Back cover: (above) Persian chinchilla cat and
          house cat
          (below) Burmese cat and black and
          white Persian cat

Photographs
Adriaanse: p. 27, upper; p. 28, upper right; p. 45;
  p. 46, upper and lower
Animal/Thompson: p. 55, upper right and lower left
Ardea/Ferero: p. 27, lower
Bielfeld: back cover, lower left
Bisserot: p. 28, upper left and lower right
Coleman/Burton: inside front cover; p. 56
Lauert: p. 18
Rinehard: front cover; inside back cover; back
  cover, upper left and right and lower right; p. 17;
  p. 28, lower left; p. 55, upper left
Schmidecker: p. 55, lower right

Contents

Cats

A Word Up Front

In this cat guide I want to inform the inexperienced cat owner about the essential things he or she needs to know to keep and care for a cat. Most important are a balanced diet, proper handling in disease or injury, and a good understanding of the cat's behavior. Also, experienced cat owners will find in this book, it is hoped, new and interesting items to complement their experience.

Mistaken (because humanized) and moralizing attitudes are still abundant. Even among cat lovers there are some who consider their cats "independent" and "self-sufficient," but decry the "servile slave behavior" of their neighbor's dog. That is wrong, and not only because it annoys the neighbor! Cats know only a limited social reference area, and their ranks are not strictly assigned. Cats make friends, but they never completely "belong." Dogs, on the contrary, have an innate sense of hierarchy because of their ancestral group life. A dog is loyal to its master, even if loyalty is undeserved, or even when the animal shows how uncomfortable it actually is with its owner!

Equally wrong is the idea that cats are "false," no matter how frequently this may still be mentioned. Cats react angrily only when they are improperly handled, or when in a bad mood, and that is quickly recognized by those who know cats. Cats expect their close "reference persons" to know the appropriate limits of action, and they expect these persons to act and think like cats. Such a person is then regarded as a type of "co-cat."

Moreover, cats are not "cruel." They consider their prey—mice or birds—just as much their meat food as we do our roast, which was once alive, too. Also, the habit of playing with the injured prey has no cruel pleasure associated, since the cat hunter is not conscious of the pain inflicted on the mouse prey. Knowledge of this pain would be a prerequisite to stimulate pleasure in cruelty.

Figure 1   *Here is a happy, well-adjusted cat greeting its master.*

There are more irrational reasons to hate cats: stubborn remainders of superstition that associated cats with witches in the Middle Ages. Even today there are otherwise knowledgeable people who feel discomfort at the sight of a black cat crossing their paths. Cats were much better off in ancient Egypt, where they were venerated as sacred animals of the goddess Bast and were respected and well treated as major fighters against mice and rats. To kill a cat then cost one's life. Cats who died were mourned and often preserved by embalming. And about Mohammed it is said that he did not wake a cat, asleep on the sleeve of his outstretched arm, even when the hour of prayer approached. He carefully cut off the sleeve and followed the prayer call.

But let's come back to the present. Only when you as a parent know how to take care of cats, will your children learn the correct ways. When we received our first kitten, I was 5 years old. That pussycat, a strong, gray tiger almost 8 weeks old, with a white throat and white paws, quickly grew accustomed to us and became an active playmate for us children. My mother had told us in advance that the kitten would not always want to play and that it needed to be undisturbed while sleeping or eating. My mother also explained that playful biting and occasional scratching were not to be considered mean. Thus no misunderstanding ensued.

Since then I have hardly had a time period without cats. I could observe much and learn more continuously. You too will recognize that you will never be bored with such house companions as temperamental, independent cats, which have a relatively high learning aptitude, provided you are willing to leave them their feline freedom.

A word about the criticism—usually from persons who do not relate to animals—to the effect that you should care for human beings in need rather than make much ado about an animal. Love, consideration, and care for animals do not preclude the same feelings for persons! In my view, both go together. One just cannot treat another creature as disposable goods.

In this book I have also incorporated the experience of other cat owners, as well as of veterinarians with whom I have had frequent and in-depth discussions. I thank all these persons at this time. Also, I owe valuable information to Professor Paul Leyhausen's writings on feline behavior and Rosmarie Wolff's book on purebred cats. Thanks also are due to the animal photographers and to Fritz Köhler for his drawings, all of whom have contributed to make the illustrations outstanding.

Finally, a remark to the parent-reader. If you are acquiring a cat mainly for your children, then give this book to them to read, as soon as they can read. I have tried to keep the text easily comprehensible in order to make the information accessible to 8- to 10-year-olds. Parents, nevertheless, serve as examples, and they need to remind children of their duties toward the cat—only because children are forgetful and because they must still learn to be responsible, considerate, and reliable.

And now I wish you much joy with your cats.

Helga Fritzsche

To Live with Cats

Ten Questions for the Conscience of the Cat Friend

When you accept an animal into your house or apartment, you must be aware of the consequences this decision entails: whether you choose a bird, a cat, or another small mammal, the animal requires space, care, and attention. You will need time, patience, and money.

So you plan to get a kitten or cat, and you want that cat to feel comfortable with you; you want it to grow and to become a happy, healthy animal which you can enjoy for a long time. In order to assure yourself that you will be able to be a good cat keeper, you should answer the following ten test questions.

If you don't answer a minimum of seven questions with an unqualified "yes," you should consider getting a different pet (goldfish, guinea pigs, or a pair of parakeets).

Question 1: Are you prepared for cat hairs on the sofa and carpet, for scratch marks on the furniture, and for the fact that your house can no longer be kept faultlessly clean?

Question 2: Can you assume that your cat will not be left alone at home longer than about 6 hours daily?

Question 3: When you keep a cat, you must be prepared to remove cat fecal matter, clean a wound that contains pus or blood, or wipe off vomited matter. Could you do all this without getting angry at the cat?

Question 4: Do the other persons in the household consent to the addition of a cat?

Question 5: Have you considered that cute, playful kittens, with childlike features and shiny blue eyes, turn into adult cats? They develop into stubborn, independent cat personalities with green or yellow eyes, that sleep all day, will not obey like dogs, and often are not willing to play.

Figure 2

Question 6: If you live in an apartment, have you made sure that your lease allows you to keep a cat?

Question 7: After you have acquired a cat, would you be willing, initially, to skip a few weekend trips to familiarize yourself with your new household member?

Question 8: Do you have relatives, friends, or neighbors who would take care of your cat while you are on vacation?

Question 9 (For adults and children): Are you able to explain to your child—to whom you want to give a kitten—that a cat requires time and attention daily? And is the child willing to sacrifice some of his or her playtime to take care of the cat? And are you willing to remind your child of these duties, when necessary?

Question 10: You cannot consistently feed a cat with leftovers from your own meals. Are you able to spend about $10-20 per month for cat food?

Considerations before the Acquisition

Domestic Cat or Purebred Cat?

You have decided to get a cat as a house companion. But what cat breed should it be: a house cat, which is called a "domestic short-hair cat" and can be bred in pedigree fashion according to coloring patterns, or can it be a mixed breed? Or would you prefer a "purebred cat" like a Persian, Burmese, Siamese, or Havannah cat, to name just a few? The purchase prices for purebred cats from breeders range from $50.00 to $300.00; alley cats or house cats you can usually expect to receive as a gift. Suggestions for locating cat breeder associations, and special breeding and care references, are listed on page 75.

In regard to intelligence and behavioral characteristics, there is a more distinct difference in character between individual cats than between different breeds. There are, however, excessively inbred "dumbbells," and deaf cats, and those that can have kittens only by Caesarian section. These cats I would advise against, even if they are prizewinners! It's a different story altogether with regard to external

Figure 3 *Consider this fact before you get a cat: long-hair cats need daily brushing.*

appearance, where each person has to decide on the basis of his or her own liking. Long-hair cats need more care than short-hair cats; they must be brushed and combed daily during their coat-change times (Figure 3), and at other times they will need brushing at least every 2-3 days. Siamese cats, like dogs, tolerate poorly the prolonged absence of their masters; they will often react with loud, interminable crying.

Where to Get the Cat of Your Choice

If you live in the city, you can buy your kitten in a pet shop or in the pet department of a department store. In a reputable pet shop kittens are kept in groups in a large cage with space to run, play, and climb, and with litterbox and basket, and they are treated with understanding based on knowledge of cat care.

If your pet shop doesn't have a kitten at the time you inquire, the shop owner will most certainly be able to acquire one for you according to your wishes. You must discuss with the owner beforehand exactly what you want: tomcat or queen (female), mixed or pure breed.

I advise against purchases from mail order catalogs. If you can get a kitten from a cat in your neighborhood, where you know the owner or the mother cat, that may be the most favorable solution.

Serious, reputable breeders (not large-scale breeders) also are usually willing to show you their animals and will be glad to talk to you to assure their kittens a good home. (There is further information on p. 75.)

Cat lovers who have knowledge and experienced animal judgment can get a kitten from a farm or from an animal shelter. With specific care, with patience, understanding, and affection, one can turn such usually neglected or fearful kittens into true house and family cats, often with especially strong, affectionate ties to their human keepers.

Age of the Animal at the Time of Purchase

A kitten should stay with its mother and littermates until it is about 8 weeks old to ensure the most favorable, healthy development.

Also, by such age the kitten will have learned considerably from its mother, for example, the danger from dogs, cars, and strange persons. This is true for relatively free-running cats, which teach their offspring by voicing warning sounds (growling). Kittens that are kept longer than 8-9 weeks with the queen will often present problems in a new environment because they have become used to their original free habitat. Frequently, these kittens may start to stray in order to find their previous surroundings, despite the love and care heaped upon them by their new owners.

Single or Double?

If you have a large apartment, house, or yard, you can easily keep two kittens, preferably littermates. Two littermate kittens know each other well and keep each other playful company, but they also need space to be able to avoid each other. It is important to allow each of them different places of quiet escape. If the kittens are brother and sister (Figure 4), make sure that they are neutered and spayed by the time they are about 7-8 months old (see p. 41).

Figure 4 *Here is how you tell male kittens from female kittens: left, male; right, female.*

Checklist for Symptoms of Diseases

Here is what you should watch for when you look for a cat or kitten:

The *coat* of a healthy kitten is soft and full, never rough, although the kitten's undercoat makes the appearance not quite as shiny as the adult cat's short-hair coat.

The *eyes* should not show signs of tearing or other discharge.

The *ears* show attention to any type of noise around the kitten. They should be clean inside. A kitten with beginning signs of ear mites or other types of ear inflammation will hold its head slightly tilted to the side and will frequently scratch the affected ear with its paws; there is a pained expression in its eyes.

If the *anus* shows signs of dried or soft fecal matter, there is evidence of diarrhea.

The whole little creature should be well rounded all over—it should not feel like a featherweight when you lift it in your hands. The belly must not be bloated, however, except right after feeding, when it may be, because some kittens are quite voracious!

Figure 5

Healthy small kittens play and "rough it" a lot—with each other, with you, with paper balls or threads, and even with their own paws, one hidden under the carpet and the other trying to catch the hidden paw. Kittens, however, take frequent snoozes during the day, often without any preliminary slowing down—they fall asleep in the midst of playing. That is normal.

If the kitten does not know you yet, it will be careful, but curious.

Sick kittens are most frequently apathetic and lethargic.

How and Where to Keep the Cat

The Indoor Territory

I mentioned before that kittens can learn
from early age to live exclusively indoors.
In that case, however, they should have the
run of the house or apartment, except
possibly the pantry. They should have all
possible available space and be free to
choose their own sleep and play areas,
provided, of course, that there are specific
pieces of cat furniture that are only for cats
(see p. 12). Since fresh air and sunlight are
of great value for a cat's good health, it is
preferable to have a balcony that can be
secured by wire mesh. If there is no
balcony, one can equally well secure a
window seat as a place in the sun and
without draft. Please make sure that the cat
can always choose between sun and shade
and that it can return into the room at any
time.

Outdoor Yards as Additional Space

A yard serves as additional space for
exercise. If you live at the edge of a
city—maybe, as I do, on a dead-end street,
where even delivery trucks move slowly,
and where fields and yards adjoin the
property—in such an environment you
should definitely let your cat run free, as
soon as an initial familiarizing time has
elapsed. Despite the cat's new
acquaintances and despite their roaming
mice hunts, there will be a close friendship
between you and your cat. If you live on a
busy street, however, the situation is
different. Fifty thousand cats are killed by
cars annually! These animals must often
endure extreme pain before they die, and
the loss always causes the owner great
sadness.

The Outdoor Kennel or Enclosure

If you plan to avoid the dangers, if you
want to raise small kittens outside without
the risk of loss, then you may choose to
have an outdoor kennel with plenty of
space, sunny and shaded areas, and play
and climbing structures. Ideally, the kennel
will adjoin the house in such a way as to
allow the cat the choice of staying indoors
or outdoors. Continuous kennel housing
without frequent personal interaction is
strongly opposed, not only by me but also
by all cat specialists. The outdoor kennel
must, of course, be covered by rustproof
wire mesh. You can choose galvanized or
coated wire material. If at all possible, you
will do well to sow grass and meadow seeds
on the ground of the kennel, preferably
before the cat arrives, to allow a dense
growth. One piece of the ground, if
available between bushes, you leave without
grass seeds; rather, you should dig the soil
over, mix it with sand or turf, and the
outdoor litterbox is ready. The sand can be
changed from time to time when necessary.

The Cat's Household Belongings

Basket

For each cat you should have a little basket, which should be upholstered with a soft pillow or blanket. Favorites are the cave baskets! The bedding should be washable. Place the basket in an area that is quiet and has no draft (Figure 6).

However, don't expect after all this that the cat will always sleep in the basket. Cats will, in no time, find other favorite sleeping places—one today, another tomorrow. That's the way cats are!

Figure 6 *Place the basket in a quiet spot.*

Litterbox and Litter

Of course, you must have a litterbox, both for the indoor and for the freely roaming cat, which has to stay indoors for some time to become familiar with the environment before being left to run free (Figure 7). Aside from this, it is advisable to let kittens use the litterbox when the weather is bad and when they do not feel well. Finally, the cat needs a clean litterbox as much as food and water when you are away for a day or even for several hours.

Figure 7 *Even cats with outdoor runs need a litterbox.*

As litter, you may best use the commonly available mineral-mix cat litter. Moist and clumps of litter can easily be removed with a small shovel, and the rest can be used again. If you keep the litter clean regularly, you can rest assured that the cat will not try to find another place to serve as bathroom; however, if the litter stays dirty, you will soon find out, because cats do not like to get their noses or paws soiled in their own excrement.

Food Bowls

Two bowls are necessary: one for dry or moist food and one for water (or milk). Because these bowls must be cleaned regularly and thoroughly, they should be of a material that is easily sanitized. Cats are strikingly sensitive to spoiled food or leftovers.

The Cat's Household Belongings

Leash

For strictly indoor cats and cats that are taken on vacation trips you will need a leash with a harness (p. 23). Practice using the leash with the kitten at as early an age as 10–12 weeks. Be patient! Don't tug and pull—a cat will never run along like a dog.

Scratch Board and Play Pole

A board or pole, covered with strong fabric, carpet, burlap, or matting, should be available to indoor as well as outdoor cats in order to provide them with a place to "sharpen" their claws; this wears them down at the same time (Figures 8 and 9). When you get such a pole or board, your furniture will be safe. To remove the claws surgically is cruel; it can be compared to removing a person's fingers down to the

knuckles. If there is enough space, you can additionally give your cat a cat tree to climb on. Most persons are handy enough

Figure 9 *Or give the cat a scratch pole covered with cloth.*

to create one. The trunk should have a circumference of about 16-20 inches, the branches should be about 20 inches long, and the surface should preferably be rough (p. 21). It is important that the tree stand safely secured. Should the tree fall accidentally, the cat may be afraid to use it again.

Figure 8 *If you want to save your furniture, give your cat, early on, a scratch board.*

13

Cat Door

If you don't enjoy getting up at all hours of the night to let your cat in or out, you should consider placing a pet door in a strategic place. The door should be of minimum size to allow your cat access but to refuse larger animals entry. Look at Figure 10 before you install your pet door. The inside should have a weather-protective folding flap, and the entry should be into an area of the house where an occasional prey mouse will not harm the floor. One can, for example, cut out a piece of window glass and replace it with the pet door. Doors leading from the pet-door entry to other rooms should be kept closed in order to avoid the possible escape of a mouse.

You should also place a basket or carton with a warm lining and food and water in the room that contains the pet door.

Figure 10 *A practical pet door and weather protection.*

Brush and Comb

For cats, especially long-hair cats, you will need a comb with wide, rounded teeth and a strong bristle brush (not wire!). The cat should be brushed and combed at regular time intervals (*best daily*). Without brushing, the cat swallows too much hair, which can lead to complications serious enough to make veterinary care necessary. When cats change their coats, they quickly look rough and neglected if they are not brushed regularly.

Short-hair cats also value being brushed despite the fact that they are usually able to take care of their own hair. During coat-changing time, it is helpful to brush the cats in order to keep the apartment or house free of cat hairs.

Adaptation to the Home and General Care

Taking the Kitten Home

Carrying the kitten home involves aggravation and stress. Choose the shortest route and avoid detours. If you have to carry the kitten, it is best kept in a strong carton with air holes or in a basket with a latch. The floor of the carrying container should be lined with plastic, a layer of newsprint, and on top a soft rag. Plastic and newsprint are necessary because kittens, no matter how clean, may get scared and will urinate. If you transport the cat in a car, you are better off with two persons; the companion should sit in the back seat with the kitten in an appropriately lined container and should gently pet the kitten and talk quietly to it. Be careful not to let the kitten crawl out of the container and accidentally end up on the driver's head or under the seat.

The First Days at Home

In the beginning, you should let the kitten run around only in one room; this room should, preferably, be the room that will later serve as main territory (first-order territory) and that from the beginning contains all the cat's belongings.

The kitten will quickly explore the room, sniffing each and every corner. Open drawers and cupboards or closets have magic attraction for kittens! Perhaps you will soon find the kitten asleep among schoolbooks or socks and underwear.

During these first days you should not leave the kitten alone for prolonged times. Cat mothers and kittens have strong ties

with each other—you must try to replace that loss initially. You can do this by petting, gently cuddling and playing, and being always aware of the unsuspecting, ignorant kitten running between your feet and trying to rub its head on your legs or to climb up them (Figure 11). Kittens are

Figure 11 *Caution, injuries! Kittens run around you unheedingly.*

unconscious of possibly life-threatening doors closing on them. One should close doors only after careful checking or should fix their openings to a certain angle (see also p. 25).

Of course, you must offer the new arrival some food and drink, preferably evaporated milk diluted one half with warm water, at about body temperature. The food you have procured is, it is hoped, similar in type to that fed in the original home; you can let a change in food occur slowly. Otherwise, try items from the list in the chapter entitled "Cat Nutrition" (p. 32).

15

Only when the kitten knows its "own" room, let it check out the rest of the house. Even later, let it try the balcony, which should, by then, be secured, or the backyard.

Seven Basic Rules for Handling Cats

1. Avoid haste, noise, and loud voices, especially in the beginning. This will facilitate the kitten's acclimatization. Also, adult cats value discipline on your part in these matters. Otherwise, cats will occasionally react with seclusion, or fearful, neurotic, nervous, or shy behavior. I have observed that cats seem to be less bothered by children's noisiness, as if they understood the difference between children and adults. Cats will frequently also tolerate children's clumsy handling, whereas they fight back when these children become older. An exception to this is the older cat, which needs quieter behavior and has acquired its own sensitive characteristics.

2. Pet and cuddle your cat, play with it, and respond to the cat's games. Don't forget that you should talk to your cat! Of course, the animal will not understand each word, but it will comprehend often-repeated words: its name (it should not be long and should be easily called), "no," "come," and, above all, the friendly sound of your voice, to which your cat will quickly respond in an equally friendly way.

3. Never lift a kitten or cat by the scruff of the neck. Lift the animals as shown in Figure 12. Some cats like to be carried like a baby, if they have been used to this since an early age—belly and all four paws up, the back resting on the person's forearm (Figure 13), like our cat Tabby.

Figure 12 *How to hold a cat properly (never loosely by the scruff of the neck!).*

Figure 13 *Some cats like this way also.*

16

4. When your cat is tired, let it sleep. This is especially important for the young kitten, which needs much sleep and cannot yet make itself understood when it needs to be left alone. Avoid having the kitten develop into a fearful cat. The children should also learn to pay attention to the kitten's needs and to play with it after it has rested and is alert and adventurous.

5. Do not disturb the cat while it is eating or drinking, or using the litterbox.

6. No cat wants to be pulled or grabbed by the tail, ears, or whiskers.

7. Ask your children to help with the care of the cat—the feeding, brushing, and also the cleaning of the food bowls and the litterbox. Children will learn consideration and reliability, although the parent remains the main keeper, who has to remind the youngsters of their duties and sometimes take over neglected tasks. A cat must be taken care of regularly and reliably.

How to Get the Cat Used to Other Pets

If you already have a dog at home, you will have very little problem, unless the dog has had bad experiences with cats and has already turned into an enemy of all cats. The proverbial dog-cat hatred is a myth, as are so many other beliefs about animal life. Animosities commonly ensue when communication is insufficient, an observation anybody can make very quickly. For example, a dog wags its tail in joyful anticipation, whereas a cat's tail moves more or less intently as concentrated observation, as well as anger and aggressiveness, increases. Dogs also sniff each other thoroughly—head to anus—upon first contact, whereas cats take much more time to get acquainted and then only carefully approach nose to nose. They react defensively to hasty approaches, which they consider aggressive: hissing, threateningly lifting one paw; the latter, however, is interpreted by the dog as a gesture to play. These are only two examples. Young dogs and cats that grow up together learn to comprehend easily and playfully each other's language. They not only live peacefully together, but also become close friends.

Figure 14 *When the dog lifts a paw, it means play, but the cat interprets this as an attack.*

A well-trained dog will quickly understand that the new kitten you brought home will now be part of the family and thus it must be treated as a friend. This is especially true if the dog does not lose attention and is continually assured of your love. I still remember our friend's giant shepherd dog, which had a pronounced penchant for aggressive escapades but considered all small creatures as his protegees who needed his specific protection. One day the family brought a new 8-week-old kitten into their home. The kitten was sitting on the kitchen floor when

19

the large dog entered, saw the new arrival, and slowly approached with friendly, wagging tail. The dog slowly lowered his nose to sniff the little creature, only to be whacked across the nose by the sharp, clawed paw of a fluffed up, frightened kitten. The dog sat back with a small shake and wagged his tail again. Within a very short time the two got along fine, and the little "archenemy" ended up sleeping in the giant's basket.

If you already have an adult cat, the development is unpredictable. Sometimes friendship ensues quickly; other times the two cats attain no more than tolerance levels. The outcome depends mostly on the nature of the older cat, because it is usual for animals to seek contact with their companions. However, a normal cat will not harm a kitten seriously. Our aged queen, Lady, initially hissed and threateningly lifted her paw at our new 5-week-old orphan kitten, Tabby. The little kitten answered by playfully rolling over on her back and remained like that until Lady left the territory. A normal adult cat does not attack a small kitten, even when dislike is obvious.

Guinea pig and rabbits will quickly get used to a kitten. They should preferably be advanced pups, young adults, or grown adults. Be sure not to leave these different animals alone with each other until you have observed that the guinea pigs and rabbits can defend themselves against the fresh behavior of the little kitten. Of course, the reverse may happen if the kitten is very young. You can help the different animals to get along more easily if you spread your attention and petting evenly over all of them. Then the adult animals will respect each other as equal companions.

A number of small animals are so tempting to cats that I have never dared to leave them alone with the felines; these are small birds, hamsters, all strains of mice, small reptiles like geckos, salamanders, and young turtles, and also frogs, toads, and fish. All these small house pets are usually kept in various types of cages, aquaria, and terraria. But you must make sure that the cat cannot paw its way into these enclosures (Figure 15), since that would be enough to jeopardize such small animals.

Figure 15 *Watch out! Cover your aquarium; some cats love fishing.*

Adaptation to the Home and General Care

Training for the Litterbox

A healthy kitten is housebroken in no time at all, provided that you supply access to an always-clean litterbox. During the first hours after the kitten's arrival, you must watch it and, as soon as it starts whimpering or moving around and searching, you lift it carefully and place it in the litterbox. Frequently, kittens understand its purpose right away, and they will urinate or defecate after a moment's scratching around in the litter. Often they will also start immediately to cover the excrement like an adult cat. Sometimes you may need to help by scratching in the sand with your fingers to show the kitten the idea. That is, usually, all there is to do. If things are not going well, however, you

Figure 16 *Cats are naturally sanitary; the anus is always cleaned.*

may not be keeping the litterbox clean enough. It is best to remove the soiled part of the litter after each use with a small scoop and replace it with clean litter whenever necessary. Once a week you should thoroughly wash and scrub the whole litterbox, and then refill it with fresh litter.

Should the stool be loose, or even watery thin, you should first examine the nutritional intake (p. 32) and then consider an underlying disease as cause (p. 36). Consequently, do not punish the

Figure 17 *A practical climbing tree for indoors: to climb on and to sharpen claws.*

kitten in a case like this, or rub its nose in the stool, which is a barbaric, inhumane method! Instead, find the cause for the diarrhea, and treat it.

A Cat's View of Furniture

If you think that upholstered furniture is comfortable and beautifies your house, and that curtains and drapes are purposeful and complementary to the design of your home, watch out: small kittens have quite different ideas about these matters. Admittedly, they appreciate the furniture as their rest places, but what could drapes and materials like wicker, fabric, and straw be better for than climbing on and sharpening claws? And, of course, they consider upholstered furniture suitable for these purposes, since it would be a waste of good opportunities if it were used only to sleep on. We are fortunate to have only one room with upholstered furniture, into which we let cats only after they are advanced in their adulthood, and even then only under initial supervision. The wicker backing of our coatrack has successfully survived 15 years and the climbing of all our diverse cats. We have always been successful in keeping the small kittens away from the curtains by attracting their attention with other toys. A few pulled threads here and there were uncomplicated enough to be easily repaired.

Good Table Manners

These words are meant literally. Small kittens can learn good manners around their food bowls quite quickly without much ado. Despite your observation that they will, initially, climb into their bowls and drip food on their coats and paws, they will quite early show their innate sense of graciousness and cleanliness. And what happens when the family sits at the dinner table? The kitten will receive a small biteful here and there; it will look so cute and funny and will soon stand on its hindlegs and wave its paws for more—and the whole family laughs and is happy. Soon the sweet

little thing jumps on chairs and table and nobody says "no."

However, when the kitten grows into a cat, then its owners usually deplore and criticize begging and tearing at the tablecloth (Figure 18), and chase the cat away. How can the cat understand this change in behavior?

Figure 18   *The dining table should be off limits to cats from early age on.*

You must know from the beginning what you will tolerate with an adult cat. Then start to enforce your wishes about behavior with consistency from the earliest age on.

Begging and jumping on the table should not be tolerated. You achieve this by feeding the cat before you have your own meals. You must also be consistent with a forceful "no" and immediately remove the kitten if it succeeds in jumping on the table from time to time before you can prevent it.

Adaptation to the Home and General Care

Cats Catch Mice and Other Things

To catch a mouse and to steal a forbidden item are the same thing in a cat's mind. Even if the cat learns that it is not allowed to "catch" certain other items, we must understand that the temptation is great, especially in unobserved moments. Resign yourself to the fact that a cat will not learn to obey exactly as a dog will. Instead of devising punishment, move the most tempting items out of reach; that goes for meats, as well as cakes or cookies, which are favorite nibbles!

Getting Used to Car and Leash

Should you intend to take your cat frequently on excursions by car, you should get the kitten used to such trips as early as possible. Start by taking the young kitten on short trips, and let it experience the car beforehand by walking around the seats and sniffing the interior. When the kitten is free in the car, there should always be a second person besides the driver. Don't leave the

Figure 19 *A cat leash for holidays and city walking.*

kitten alone in the car for longer than one-half hour. Park the car in a shady place and leave the windows open, enough to air the car, but not enough to let the kitten escape. Watch out! If the cat can fit its head through, the whole body can squeeze through, too! If the cat leaves the car in a strange environment, it will get scared and react improperly by hiding in a place where you cannot find it again, or it may be killed by a passing car.

It is practical to use a harness and leash for short trips in the immediate neighborhood (Figure 19). You should get the cat used to this as early as possible, preferably by 3 months of age. When you train your kitten on a leash in your backyard, play with the kitten and be patient. Don't pull on the leash, and take the kitten frequently in your arms for a moment of assurance.

Unfortunately, not all cats react the same to a leash, and this good advice is not always followed by success. The individual temperament of each cat will ultimately determine the result.

What to Do When a Neighbor Complains

Since I know that pets, including cats, can spoil good neighborly relations, I want to help you avoid this. Good neighborly relations are worth preserving, bad neighborly relations ought to be improved—and both of these endeavors are also in your cat's interest.

Bone of Contention 1: Your cat has just used your neighbor's freshly seeded flower

23

bed as a bathroom. Explain to your neighbor that, unfortunately, cats appreciate a dry, sandy "toilet," and that the cat will not use the ground if he will keep it moist, which is better for the seeds and disliked by the cat. As soon as the plants are larger, the cat will no longer use the place.

Bone of Contention 2: The cat has been watching birds at the neighbor's birdbath and birdhouse. Now the cat has tried to get birds from the birdhouse, or young birds from the nest. Explain that human evaluation of this animal behavior is a false extrapolation of human moral values. Tell

your neighbor that you want to help with the problem by making bird catching more difficult for your cat: a birdhouse is best placed on a post approximately 2 yards high, which is too thin and too smooth to climb, and too light to jump on. You can also suggest planting a rose bush at the pole and winding the branches around the pole; that will definitely discourage any cat from climbing. Birdbaths are best placed next to trees or bushes that do not obstruct the view and are not too far for escape, because a wet bird moves more slowly. Pine trees and beautifully blooming thorny bushes (wild and garden rosebushes, and other plants with thorns that one can find in the nursery; Figure 20) provide great protection for hatching and young birds. Bird nests on trees can be protected by a collar of thorns around the trunk of the tree. Cats avoid and hate everything that may tear or pull their hair coat. A tip for you: Offer your practical help to your neighbor to prepare and construct these items to discourage your cat. Such an offer usually helps to soften the initially angry reaction of the neighbor.

Bone of Contention 3: Your cat has watched, scared, or even injured animals in an outdoor bird cage, a run, an outdoor terrarium or aquarium, or a garden pond. To solve this problem, you will need some time, especially if the neighbor is not willing to attend to the matter himself. Buy a toy pistol, watch your cat, and shoot it with water just when it is ready to sneak up on the animals in question. You must not be seen by your cat, in order to discourage it from that specific action. If the cat can

Figure 20 *A flowering thorny plant serves as protection for a birdhouse.*

see you, it will quickly find out that it has only to wait until you are no longer or not yet present.

Bone of Contention 4: The neighbor complains that your cat—how ill-mannered!—has left its feces on his or her front lawn. Try to be courteous when you explain that cats distinctly dislike lawns to leave their feces on, since cats need to cover their excrement, and that they don't like to be in plain view while they go to the bathroom. Explain that the mysterious fecal remains stem from a small dog or perhaps a hedgehog but never from your cat. Your dog should be walked for that purpose in order not to cause these problems. The small amount of feces that could be left by a hedgehog can be considered lawn food!

. . . And Some Public Relations

There are all kinds of mice in many yards and gardens. These animals often cause your neighbor more anger than your cat does. Therefore, when you converse across the garden fence, remember to mention frequently that your cat just caught a mouse, or perhaps just emptied a whole nest of mice! Of course, it would be even better if you could watch your cat catch a mouse in your neighbor's garden. That would at least result in respect for the "mouse killer" in your cat.

Accidents, Indoors and Outdoors

This is an especially important matter as long as your kitten is small and inexperienced, and it is not unimportant when your cat is grown.

● It is hard to eradicate the old wives' tale that cats always land on their feet, no matter where and how far they fall. Surely, cats are agile and quick in their reactions. (Exceptions are cat babies and old and sick cats.) But their bone structure is fragile, and they can easily fracture bones with just a fall from a balcony or a window one floor high. That is why you should secure your balcony and window, possibly with a wire-mesh screen (Figure 21), or let your cat sit only at a closed window.

Figure 21 *The safe balcony: ideal for apartment cats, which must be left alone for prolonged time periods.*

● Kittens play with everything that attracts their attention; that includes electric wires. For your own and your cat's sake, you should move these wires out of reach.
● Young kittens crash from nowhere between your legs, topple with persistence

around your feet, and jump (without warning) at your legs and try to climb up. Be careful, then, to watch constantly where you walk in order to avoid injuring the little animal that has adopted you as its mother.

● Sometimes kittens decide in a fraction of a moment to rush after you, just when you are ready to close a door. Therefore it is best that you always turn to check and fix open doors so that they won't shut on the kitten. If a kitten gets caught in a closing door, there is the risk of serious back injury and untreatable paralysis.

● Free-running outdoor cats are seriously endangered by street traffic. Consequently, if you live near a busy street, you may want to consider raising your cat exclusively indoors, or you may prefer an outdoor run, which can be secured on all sides and on top, too, and can be used by the cat at its own will rather than as a forced containment.

● Many items used every day in house and yard are equally dangerous for small children and for small animals; and they should, therefore, be placed out of reach: cleaning disinfectants, insecticide chemicals, mouse and vermin poisons, sprays of all kinds. Mouse and rat traps belong to this group, too. Also, the laundry and dishwashing machines must be checked before you use them, because your cat may have climbed inside and fallen asleep in this cozy, dark, warm place. It should be expected that pins, needles, beads, and small balls will not be left lying about, for they may be swallowed.

Cat Care during Vacations

I'm sure you are not one of those who remember their pets just moments before they leave for vacations. Certainly you also detest the methods such persons use to deal with their dilemma: euthanasia or abandonment.

Vacation time needs as much planning for our pets as it does for ourselves.

Contrary to the often repeated statement that cats are wild animals capable of self-sufficiency, I want to emphasize that cats are domestic, house-bound animals that are more sensitive than their wild counterparts and depend on dry, warm quarters with human attention and measured nutrition, no matter how many mice they may catch. This is true also for cats that are raised outdoors and run free.

Queens that are pregnant or are feeding their kittens should not be left alone, nor should they be taken along on a vacation trip.

When You Leave for a Day's Trip

You can leave your cat alone for 1 day as long as you provide enough food and water. Leave, also, a clean litterbox. Free-running cats may be left with access to a building through a door or window left ajar or a pet door, at least in cases where this can be considered safe.

Where to Place the Cat during Vacation

When you leave for days or weeks, you must decide how you want to provide for the cat:

- To leave the cat in your house under the care of a familiar, reliable, and understanding person
- To give the cat to a reliable, familiar, and understanding person for care in his or her house
- To place the cat in a pet hotel or boarding kennel
- To take the cat along on your vacation

The most suitable solution for cats is the first choice above. Most cats dislike travel and environmental change. When the person who takes care of the cat (twice daily) is known to you and your cat and knows that proper care includes feeding, talking, petting, and playing, all is well. When the cat doesn't know the new caretaker very well, there may be some problems in store, as happened once with our cat: the helpful woman was attacked and could accomplish her cat-care duties only with difficulty. I hold her in high regard for having kept her commitment under such circumstances. When the same woman had visited us previously, she and the cat had always been friends; but when we left the house, our cat Lady behaved like a watch dog.

An indoor cat will usually tolerate staying with another, preferably familiar, family. Despite the stress of changes in environment and personal care, this is definitely a better choice than placing the cat in an animal boarding home. I do not generally recommend boarding kennels, no matter how well they are run, because they are not compatible with the basic cat nature, and also they are usually filled to capacity during vacation times.

29

Traveling with a Cat

Some cats suffer more seriously than others when they are left alone. They eat less or stop eating altogether. They may become fearful and start walking about in widening circles to search for their "lost" environment. I, sadly enough, experienced this some time ago. The best solution to this problem is separate vacations for various family members, but that works only for families with grown children.

The second-best solution is to take the cat along on your vacation. Of course, not all cats travel well, even when quiet cat facilities are available. You will do best to experiment with a trip of short duration. Your cat should become travel experienced, quiet, and not excitable. Remember that camping trips are torture for any cat, and exclude the cat from such vacations.

Cat Baggage

Figure 22 *Cat basket for travel and visits to the veterinarian.*

Baggage for the traveling cat includes the familiar basket (Figure 22) or, at least, the familiar blanket, the usual dry food, the familiar food bowls, and the litterbox with litter and scoop.

Traveling by Car or Public Conveyance

Now, please, read again the beginning of the chapter "Adaptation to the Home and General Care" (p. 15), where you will find all you need to know about the transport box and what to do during the trip. You should realize the stress a prolonged automobile trip inflicts on a cat—the shaking in the car, the heat or cold, and the excitement of any environmental changes. It is best if one family member can keep the transport box or basket on his or her lap. Never place the container close to the heater outlet. The transport container should give the cat enough room to sit and lie down, but no more.

Keep a harness and leash close by, and walk the cat during a break every 1–2 hours, which will benefit the human being as much as the animal. Walk the cat for a few moments away from highway noises and large numbers of people. Then offer some food and water each time.

For traveling with your cat by plane, train, or bus you should request the transportation regulations ahead of your travel date. Approved containers are available for purchase (e.g., at the airline ticket counter), or you may bring your own if it satisfies the standards. The cat-carrying box must fit under the seat. If it is too

Cat Care during Vacations

large, you will have to leave it in the luggage compartment.

You may not let the cat out of the container except during stopovers. For these occasions you should be equipped with leash and litterbox. I advise you to take two strong plastic bags, one for plenty of clean litter and one for the scoop and the soiled litter.

When you travel to a foreign country, you must inquire—several months ahead—about the health certification required for that country and for your return to the United States. Each country has different requirements for quarantine, vaccinations, and health certificates. These requirements change from time to time. You can obtain information from the country's consulate general, from your state veterinarian's office (USDA), and from your veterinarian.

At the Vacation Destination

Cats will usually react with instinctive care in a new environment. Frequently they may be frightened. In the beginning leave your cat only in the rented room, and do not leave the animal alone for too long. When you open windows or doors, put your cat on the leash. Once the cat has discovered all corners of the room and has found its familiar belongings from its luggage, it will usually become quiet and normally calm.

Later you can try taking your cat on the leash for a walk outdoors. But do not insist when you know that there are dogs around, or when you notice that the animal cannot overcome fear despite your presence and a safe environment.

Cat Nutrition

The short-hair cat has developed as a domestic cat from the North African tabby cat and the European wildcat. They are closely related and were mixed early on before they were brought to this country.

Wildcats feed almost exclusively on live small mammals that are eaten and digested completely, including the stomach contents, such as seeds, greens, and grains, which may be fresh or partially digested. Thus they consume, apart from the protein and fat of the meat, also carbohydrates, vitamins, and trace elements. The digestive tract of the domestic cat is hardly different from that of the wildcat. The nutrition of domestic cats, then, must also consist of sufficient animal protein, fat, some carbohydrates, vitamins, and trace elements.

What Counts

You must be conscious of the nutritional requirements mentioned above, especially if your cat is kept strictly indoors. If, of course, you feed commercial catfood exclusively, you need not worry, for the available prepared catfoods are usually mixed to contain all of the normally required components of cat nutrition. It is important that you never feed food straight from the refrigerator, for cats have quite sensitive stomachs. Cold or overstored food can easily cause digestive disturbances. Free-roaming cats know just how much food they need to eat; and, unlike dogs, cats stop eating when they are no longer hungry. Overfeeding or overeating is a problem that arises mainly with indoor cats.

Just as frequently happens with human beings, these cats are inclined to overeat and become overweight when they are bored. In that case you must decide on the appropriate portion of food, and not allow your cat to develop a big tummy.

What Cats Drink

Sufficient fresh, clean water must be provided at all times and for all cats, young and old. Fill the water bowl daily. Remember: Milk is a food and not a drink to replace water!

If your cat still likes milk as a grown cat, you can give it evaporated milk, which should be diluted with one-third lukewarm water. Fresh whole milk may also be used.

What Cats Eat

Cats that run free in rural areas get most of their meat meals from catching mice. All other cats must be fed according to their needs. Most cats like a certain amount of variation in their meals, and for these cats there is an abundance of commercial catfoods. These foods are especially convenient when you are on vacation, whether you have the cat with you or leave it with your friends. With this type of prepared foods, even the novice at cat care will not make mistakes, since all nutrients are premixed and contained in the packaged product. Dry food is especially helpful to keep teeth and gums in good condition and to avoid buildup of tooth tarter. That is reason enough to feed it frequently, but not in large amounts. I give my cats dry cat biscuits from time to time, which they like very much. Remember that you must always offer plenty of water with dry foods.

Wildcats and free-running cats are often seen eating grass. Small amounts of grass help these cats to regurgitate and emit hair balls that have formed in their stomachs as a result of their grooming habits. When hair balls accumulate in the stomach, they can cause serious disease in the cat. Long-hair cats must be brushed and combed no matter how much grass they have access to. Greens are also essential for indoor cats. They should have greens available to nibble on and possibly derive certain nutrients from. You can seed "cat grass" in pots or flats. Seeds for grass are available in nurseries. Or you can have some pots of green lillies (*Chlorophytum*) in the house; they are just what a cat likes and they are highly digestible. Be sure not to spray these plants with insecticides, and keep the cat away when you spray other plants!

Correct Amounts of Food

Adult cats (starting at 9 months of age) need one or two meals per day: a total of 300 calories (see the table on p. 35).

Old cats, which have lost some or most of their teeth, need three or four small meals. If you do not feed canned food, you must cut meat into very small pieces or break it up in a mixer or blender to a soft consistency. Add fresh water.

Cats with little exercise, especially spayed and neutered cats, get fat easily. You must cut the food portion and not allow a big belly to develop!

Pregnant cats will frequently show increased appetite. If they have enough exercise, you may increase their food portions and offer them four small meals. But watch out that the cat doesn't become fat, since that could cause difficulty at the time of delivery. Indoor as well as outdoor cats that are not fed commercial catfood must receive calcium supplements in their nutrition. Your veterinarian can recommend the correct type and amount. Follow the veterinarian's instructions exactly. When a cat catches mice regularly, there is less need for calcium supplements.

Lactating cats also need more and highly nutritional food in three or four portions per day. Prepared products are preferable to assure nutritional balance.

Kittens feed on mother's milk for about 8-9 weeks. However, you should offer them supplemental food from the time they are about 5 weeks old. If the mother's food is not suitable for kittens, you may feed them oatmeal or other cereal cooked in diluted evaporated milk (or fresh whole milk). Or you may use one of several types of mother-replacement milk (e.g., Similac or KMR), which you can get from the veterinarian, the pet store, or the supermarket. This can be mixed with a small quantity of chopped meat, which you should warm to body temperature in your hands before you feed it. Uncoordinated young kittens can lick this food from your fingers more easily than from a bowl.

Orphan kittens: If the mother cat dies or if you decide to raise an orphan kitten (abandoned kittens are only too frequently found), you must thoroughly consider your decision. It takes much energy and trouble to raise orphan kittens. Before you decide whether the kitten(s) should be humanely put to death by a veterinarian or whether you choose to invest much time, care, and loving attention, you must know what you are in for! Kittens under the age of 2 weeks are excessively difficult to raise to become healthy adults. However, even older kittens present difficult feeding patterns as long as they would naturally still feed from the mother. Kittens are hard to convince to drink from a small baby bottle. They usually won't feed from a flat bowl until they are at least 3 or, more likely, 4 weeks old. You can try to feed them from a small teaspoon. Up to 10 days of age the kittens must be fed every 2–3 hours, including nights. Later you can prolong the night intervals but not to exceed 5-6 hours. This must continue until the kittens feed themselves in appropriate quantities.

The orphan kittens must also be kept warm in their basket: a wrapped hot-water bottle will do the job; it must never be hot, however, but always be warm. The young kittens require also, after each meal, that you massage their little bellies gently in order to evacuate their bladders and intestines. The contents must then be removed. As important as feeding are petting, talking, cuddling, and playing. Orphan kittens will usually accept canned

food as early as 3–4 weeks after birth. You may have to hand-feed the first few bites in order to accustom them to the flavor and consistency (Figure 23).

Figure 23 *Another possible way to feed solid food to young kittens.*

Well-kept, well-fed kittens are round and solid all over without being fat or skinny; they have a shiny hair coat and look at you with alert and clear eyes.

Incorrectly fed kittens show a dull hair coat and dull eyes. If they have been fed too much or exclusively liver, growth problems may be apparent, as well as improper bone development, and internal hemorrhaging or vomiting may occur.

Cat Nutrition

Suggestions for the Correct Feeding of Cats

Age	Meals per Day	Body Weight (pounds)	Food Intake (ounces)	Daily Calories	Meal Suggestions
Birth to 6th week	Kitten is fed by mother.				
6–8 weeks	6	1	5	150	Suggestions I, II, III
3rd month	5	2	7	200	Suggestions I, II, III
4th month	4	$2\frac{1}{2}$	8	230	Suggestions I, II, III, $1\frac{1}{2}$ times amount
5th month	3	3	9	260	8 oz. canned food + $\frac{1}{2}$ oz. oatmeal or rice
6th month	2	4	10	291	9 oz. canned food + $\frac{1}{2}$ oz. oatmeal or rice
7th month	2	5	$11\frac{1}{2}$	310	11–12 oz. canned food or dry food as desired
8–11 months	1–2	5	11	300	3 oz. canned food + $\frac{1}{2}$ oz. oatmeal or rice plus dry food as desired
		$5\frac{1}{4}$	$10\frac{1}{2}$	290	
		$5\frac{1}{2}$	$10\frac{1}{2}$	290	
		6	10	280	

Daily calories necessary for adult cats (1 or 2 meals):
  6 pounds body weight: 250 cal.
  8 pounds body weight: 320 cal.
  10 pounds body weight: 350 cal.

Suggestion I: 1 boiled egg, 1 Tbs. canned food, $\frac{1}{2}$ oz. oatmeal or rice (160 cal.).
Suggestion II: 2 oz. canned food, mixed with: 2 crackers, some vegetables (2 oz.), 1 tsp. vegetable oil; you may add some evaporated milk (170 cal.).
Suggestion III: 2 Tbs. canned food, 2 oz. evaporated milk, 1 handful cornflakes, 2 oz. mashed vegetables (175 cal.).

Offer some grass to nibble on or *Chlorophytum* (p. 33), starting in 7th week.

When the Cat Is Sick

Cats are generally quite resistant to infectious diseases, provided they were kept and nourished properly during their infancy and growth to adulthood. There is, however, no absolute assurance against disease. The major two diseases, distemper and rabies, can affect all cats, even the best fed, strongest, and healthiest ones. Fortunately, vaccines are available to protect your cats from these infectious diseases. In your own and your cat's interest you should see to it that your cat is vaccinated.

Distemper

Distemper is a serious disease with a group of symptoms caused by a viral infection: diarrhea, severe respiratory problems, and blood dyscrasias. Fever will accompany these symptoms in most cases, and it is typical to observe the third eyelid over part of the nasal aspect of the eyes (Figure 24).

Figure 24 *External signs of distemper: the third eyelid stays pulled up over part of the eye even though the eye is open.*

Weakness, lack of appetite, and lethargy are also part of the disease syndrome.

If the disease is treated by a veterinarian early at the onset, there is a fair chance of recovery. However, there may remain complications that can last for weeks and months. An example is diarrhea, which forces a cat to lose its stool without control and which can be cured only by veterinary treatment and with much care and patience.

If the cat is not treated with medication, there is only a 5 percent chance of survival. Kittens should be first vaccinated at about 8 weeks of age, a booster should follow at about 12 weeks of age, and yearly boosters should be received thereafter.

Rabies

This disease cannot be treated or cured in either human being or animal. The course of the disease and the terminal agony are tragic. Unless your cat is to be kept strictly indoors, you should have the kitten initially vaccinated at about 3–6 months of age and should provide booster shots every year. The veterinarian will issue a certificate for each vaccination. This vaccination certificate is of importance for a trip to a foreign country, and it also serves as a reminder of the date for the booster shots.

If you have an outdoor-roaming cat, you should beware of rabies-infested areas. Depending on the state and country you live in, your cat may be caught and killed if rabies is endemic in the area.

When the Cat Is Sick

Other Important Diseases

Cat Flu
This group of respiratory diseases is caused by viruses. Sneezing and runny eyes may be symptoms. Have your cat vaccinated against these viral diseases at the time of the distemper shots.

Feline Infectious Peritonitis
General symptoms of disease may be present. A veterinarian has to send blood to a laboratory to test for this disease, which is caused by a virus and can be fatal. No vaccine is yet available

Cat Leukemia (Feline Leukemia Virus Disease)
This leukemia is infectious only to cats. Symptoms may be weight loss, anemia, and lethargy. Your veterinarian can test your cat for this disease. There is no vaccine yet available.

Parasitic Diseases
There are many parasites, internal and external, that can affect your cat. If there is any evidence of worms, fleas, or ear mites, get specific medication from your veterinarian. Do not experiment with drugs prescribed for other animals since most parasites are very host-specific.

Are Cat Diseases Dangerous to the Owner?

A healthy owner is usually not affected by organisms that cause cat diseases. However, extra cleanliness and scrupulous hygiene should be observed if your cat is sick or shows any symptoms of unknown origin. Owners who are sick themselves, are in fragile health, are very old, or are otherwise unusually susceptible should be especially careful in handling their cat's excrements or discharges during the course of an illness.

Symptoms of Diseases

If you know your cat well and observe it closely, you will recognize any changes that may occur in its behavior or appearance. Of course, such symptoms do not provide you with a diagnosis of the disease. Typical warning signals are lack of appetite (anorexia), excessive need to rest, increased thirst, and diarrhea.

The body temperature is frequently raised when the causes are of serious nature. The normal body temperature of a cat is 101-103°F (38-39.5°C). If the cat's temperature passes 103°F (39.5°C), you should call the veterinarian immediately. You measure your cat's temperature rectally. To do this you will need a helper, who restrains the cat by holding the front paws and shoulder area, while talking quietly and assuringly to the cat. Watch out that the thermometer does not slide out or break if you use a glass thermometer. Dip the (small) thermometer into some salad oil before you insert the end carefully into the rectum. Read the temperature after about 2 minutes.

Cats are difficult patients. When they feel ill, they will often not trust their closest human friends, and they will try to escape.

You have to understand this characteristic and try to be firm without being hurtful. It takes a firm, assured grip when injuries need bandaging or medication is to be given. If you feel that you cannot restrain your cat properly, you should ask your veterinarian for help.

Injuries and Fractures

Small injuries, as well as partial fractures, heal amazingly quickly without much assistance. When injuries are more serious, you should contact a veterinarian immediately. Even very serious injuries rarely require euthanasia. Our cat Misty once lost two toes when she got caught in our neighbor's harvesting machine. We took her immediately to the veterinarian, and under anesthesia he amputated one whole and one half toe and bandaged the paw. The injury healed very quickly, and Misty could soon climb trees just as well as ever.

Figure 25 *Bandage for injured or broken paw.*

I do recommend, however, that you always get advice from a veterinarian if the injury or symptom does not improve or disappear after 1 or 2 days, no matter how minor it may appear.

Common Health Problems

Diarrhea may be a rather harmless result of indigestion due to overfeeding liver, spleen, or milk, or to ingestion of some stale catfood. Cats are quite sensitive in this respect. You may offer your cat some diluted tea to drink and plain chopped meat to eat. It is best to add a small amount of Kaopectate or other antidiarrhea drug from your pharmacy or pet store. If there is no improvement after 1 or 2 days, you must consult a veterinarian, as there may be a serious cause for the symptom.

Constipation can be recognized when the cat tries unsuccessfully to eliminate stool despite straining; or when the cat passes small, hardened pieces of stool with signs of pain. You can treat your cat with a teaspoonful of mineral oil (never use castor oil!).

Vomiting is not necessarily serious. Typical harmless examples are regurgitation of hair balls or chunks of meat that were eaten too quickly. The occurrence of hair balls can be minimized by regular brushing and combing. This is especially important for long-hair cats and during the change of coat twice a year. Intestinal worm infestation is also a major cause of vomiting. Usually you can recognize the typical thin, threadlike worms in the discharged contents. The veterinarian will provide you with appropriate medication to treat your cat for these parasites. If your

When the Cat Is Sick

cat should vomit several times in one day without apparent cause, you should consult a veterinarian as soon as possible.

Urine retention can have serious consequences. You must seek veterinary attention immediately. This problem occurs more frequently in older, neutered tomcats. You recognize the symptom when you see that the cat fails to eliminate despite straining.

Dull or rough hair coat is always an indication of poor general condition. If you are sure that the cat receives proper nutrition and is free of intestinal worms, you should check the body temperature. If the cat is running a fever, you must get veterinary attention, since serious diseases could be the cause of these symptoms.

Eye infections are more frequently seen in young kittens. About 10 days after birth, when the eyelids open, you will observe that the kittens show swollen eyelids and mucinous, pussy discharge, often encrusted. You should clean the eyes by wiping them carefully with a soft handkerchief or washcloth (never cotton balls) soaked in lukewarm water (no medication is necessary). This should be done daily as required. If the discharge continues for several days, you should consult a veterinarian.

Earaches and ear itching may be caused by ear mites or also by a cold or flu. Cats react to this symptom by scratching their ears with their paws (Figure 26), by frequently flattening out their ears, or by rubbing them on the floor or against objects. If you can see some dark-stained material inside the ear, you must get proper medication from the veterinarian. The first ear treatment should best be performed by the veterinarian to show you how to go on from there. It takes know-how and patience.

Figure 26 *When a cat scratches one or both ears, you should suspect ear mite infestation.*

Tapeworm infestation is not infrequent in outdoor cats. This type of tapeworm is specific to cats only. You can recognize the typical small, whitish, flat egg packets (glottids) around the anus, the root of the tail, on the cat's resting place, or in the stool. These tapeworm parts are shiny moist at first and dried later. The veterinarian will prescribe specific medication that will enable the cat to eliminate this parasite.

Ticks can make life miserable for many animals, outdoor cats included. Ticks attach to the skin of the cat by biting and sucking blood. They also transmit diseases. To loosen the grip of this parasite, you can drop some salad oil on the tick, which will release its bite and fall off, or you can pull the tick off the skin quite easily with a pair of forceps (Figure 27). It is essential that you grip the tick as closely to the skin as possible in order to assure that you will pull the tick's head out of the skin rather than breaking it off.

Figure 27 *Here is how to remove ticks: talk to the animal with reassuring voice while you use the forceps.*

Fleas can transmit diseases also. Cat fleas are specific for cats, and will not stay on other animals for any length of time. When your cat needs a flea treatment, be sure to get a safe spray or powder or to ask your veterinarian. Cats groom themselves constantly, so that the flea medication must be specifically safe for cats. Use spray or powder on the cats (protect their eyes) as well as on their resting places. Wash their pillows or blankets. If the fleas are all over the house, you should use time-release sprays. All of the procedures should be repeated after 5-8 days to kill newly hatched eggs.

Rheumatism does not seem to occur frequently in cats; at least I have not found much about it in the available literature on these animals. It does exist, however. Our cat Misty frightened us one day when she started screaming and growling as I touched her paws. She had always loved being petted, and I suspected that she might have rabies. However, the veterinarian told me that Misty suffered from rheumatism. He gave me some medication for her, and she felt fine just a few days later. We were puzzled how rheumatism could possibly affect an animal inside a fur coat!

Surgery

Before any surgery (e.g., spaying or neutering) you have to fast your cat to prevent the animal from vomiting after the surgery. The veterinarian will tell you exactly how long before the surgery the cat may have food and drink. Write this information down at the time you fix the date for the surgery. If you have an outdoor cat, you should keep it indoors a day before the surgery, because, if left outdoors, the cat may find another appetizing mouse before surgery time, or may decide to hide when the time to leave for the surgery approaches.

If your cat is used to car travel, a friend can hold it—of course, in the back seat—and talk to it assuringly. Otherwise you should put the cat in a safely locked but well-ventilated container (p. 15). After surgery the cat is best left in its own basket in a quiet, draft-free, warm room. Keep the litterbox close by. When the anesthetic has worn off and the cat is fully awake, you should offer it fresh and sufficient drinking water.

You will hear about surgical removal of the cat's front claws from time to time. I consider this procedure cruel and inhumane and discourage its application strongly. Secondary infections can occur, and the cat can no longer climb and hold on. People who want a cat without claws should get a stuffed toy cat.

Neutering and Spaying

Neutering a tomcat (castration, removal of the testicles) is a routine surgical procedure for a small-animal practitioner. It is done, of course, under anesthesia appropriate for cats. A healthy tomcat recovers quickly from this procedure. Neutered toms will stop "spraying" their territory, a result that is especially important for owners of indoor animals. The neutered tom also strays less, gets into fewer fights, and thus risks his life much less often than toms that stray and mate. The neutered tomcat also reduces the unwanted cat population, a problem that causes much misery for many cats.

Spaying queens (sterilization, removal of ovaries and uterus, hysterectomy) is major surgery of the abdominal cavity. However, it is also routine surgery for a veterinarian who specializes in small-animal practice. A healthy female cat, which was kept properly before and after the surgery, will be up and about 1 week after the surgery.

Some queens will be in heat more than twice per year. It is not uncommon that queens which are kept strictly indoors may be in heat every 6 weeks; they will make prolonged, noisy lamentations if they are not let out of the house and will try to escape on every occasion. If you do let them out, you must expect at least two

litters per year, each of which may consist of six kittens. Too often there is no quick decision made to provide immediate and humane euthanasia after birth, and too often these kittens end up suffering inhumane conditions and cruel deaths. Sometimes owners get rid of kittens by giving them to people they do not know; sometimes they abandon kittens; and sometimes the kittens end up in an animal shelter to relieve the owner's bad conscience. Despite the good treatment provided in an animal shelter, cats cannot be happy there because they live, without territory, in groups and in cages, and they must be killed after a short time if they are not placed in homes. The best way to dispose of unwanted kittens is humane euthanasia by a veterinarian. Never drown kittens! Even when they are placed in a sack with stones and drowned, the agony of death is cruelly prolonged. When no veterinarian is at hand, a quick death can be caused by a well-aimed, hard blow on the head. I have given this subject special attention to underline the importance of spaying or neutering your cats! Only this step can help prevent the countless unnecessary and cruel deaths that still abound.

Spayed and neutered cats remain just as temperamental and playful as their whole counterparts of the same age group provided they are not overfed or excessively restricted in their exercise. These cats also continue catching mice when they have the opportunity. It is certainly not appropriate to keep cats that must continuously be restrained from their mating behavior patterns, a restriction that often turns into torture for both animals and owners. If, however, you know at least one or two persons who would like a kitten, and if you would like to raise one for yourself, then you should let your cat have kittens once before she is spayed (see p. 48). Many cat owners, experienced in raising cats, agree that some cats which are spayed early may turn out to be more nervous and more easily scared than cats that have had a litter at least once.

Painless Euthanasia

When a cat suffers from an incurable disease, it is acceptable and even recommended to have a veterinarian "put the animal to sleep." Modern drugs allow this type of euthanasia to proceed painlessly and similarly to falling asleep. The cat will be calmer and less frightened if a familiar person stays with it during the procedure, if this is acceptable to the veterinarian's practicing protocol.

The Cat's Medicine Cabinet

A safely locking box or a separate small cabinet is best suited for your cat's medical supplies. Do not use your family's medicine cabinet for the cat's medications and utensils! Also, do not experiment on the cat with your family's drugs when the cat is ill! Animals are sensitive to particular drugs and must be treated with specifically prescribed medications. Just as children's medications should be kept away from them, you should also keep your cat's medicine out of reach of the animal.

This should be the contents of the cat's medicine cabinet:
- A good pair of scissors with rounded points
- A pair of forceps with rounded points.
- A small, unbreakable thermometer.
- Broad Band-aids and tape.
- Cotton.
- Sterile gauze.
- Petroleum jelly (Vaseline).
- Boric acid.
- A bottle of saline (commercially available).
- All medications prescribed by your veterinarian for your cat. Keep only medications that are legibly labeled and have not expired. Other medication should be discarded. The veterinarian can tell you the expiration date and the necessary storage instructions for each drug.
- The phone number and address of your veterinarian.

In order to treat your cat with correct dosages of liquid medication, you should familiarize yourself with spoon and cup measures:

1 ml = 15 drops	1 glass = 8 oz. (240 ml)
1 tsp. = 4–5 ml	1 measuring cup = ½
2 Tbs. = 30 ml	pint = 240 ml
1 teacup = 6 oz. (180 ml)	2 measuring cups = 1 pint = 500 ml = ½ liter

Treating cats and giving them medicine orally is often difficult. You may need a helper to restrain the cat or to open its mouth to introduce the medication. If you have an excessively difficult patient, you may need help from the veterinarian. In some cases the veterinarian will inject the cat with enough of a tranquilizing drug to complete the necessary procedure.

The Cat Family

Preface

Before deciding to fulfill one's understandable wish for a cat family, sober considerations are necessary and clear decisions have to be made: better to decide against it, including all its consequences, such as sterilization or castration (p. 41), than to go along with the more comfortable thought that "things will take care of themselves," at a cost the animals will ultimately have to pay.

The question of how to shelter and house a litter of kittens is often difficult to answer when dealing with the common house cat, and even with purebred cats this aspect is not altogether without its problems. Each kitten needs people who understand animals; it needs sufficient space and proper care and feeding. When these are provided, the kitten can live its life according to its intended life span. Without them, it would be better off not to have been born. Anonymous sales through third parties, without one's own knowledge of the future owner, ought therefore not to exist. Perhaps sometimes the opportunity exists to find appropriate "parents" by beginning the search among one's acquaintances or looking through classified ads either before or immediately after the birth of the new litter. But you must use caution and common sense! When someone genuinely likes animals, he or she will understand any misgivings or questions you may have and will keep an open mind with respect to any advice. Certainly you yourself should be able to understand that a potential cat owner may want to observe cats and kittens in their customary surroundings, as well as—in the case of purebred cats—to check documents concerning lineage and necessary shots. Use this time as an opportunity to check out the potential buyer while he or she observes and handles the animals—this is definitely to the buyer's advantage, as well as yours and the kittens'.

"Cats and kittens in their customary surroundings"—these words lead me to another point that should be made: each cat family needs sufficient space as well as sufficient appropriate, nutritionally balanced food. It needs your daily attention and care. Forget about short trips and vacations shortly before the birth of the litter and especially during the initial growing stages of the kittens!

To ensure that you, as the would-be owner of a purebred cat, really receive a pedigreed animal, your cat needs a certified pedigree. Fees for breeding do not come inexpensively; they range somewhere between $50.00 and $300.00

If you are planning to win prizes at shows with your animal, please consider that this is not easily accomplished. Know that each show with all its accompanying turmoil means considerable stress for the animal, as well as time and money as far as you are concerned. Keep this in mind if you intend to breed cats in order to achieve a profit, or if you covet special honors.

If, however, after carefully reading this preface and considering all conditions, you still want to proceed with a litter for your cat, or even with the breeding of purebred cats, because you are convinced that you are suited to do this and are able to satisfy all of the above conditions, and also because you are especially fond of one or the other species, then this chapter on the cat family becomes of special importance to you. On p. 75 you will find a list of books under the heading "Books to Enhance Your Knowledge and Understanding of Cats."

Love Play of Cats

Domestic cats mature and are able to mate at about 8 months of age. At that time have them spayed or neutered. Do not proceed with castration or sterilization before this age, as the animals have not fully developed and after surgery will not continue to grow or may grow without achieving correct proportions (e.g., the head may remain too small).

When a female cat (queen) is in heat, it may express this in restlessness, a marked need for affection, an aromatically scented hair coat ("perfumed for the tomcat," we used to say as children), head rubbing (p. 57), and, finally, a rhythmic, truly flirtatious rolling back and forth on her back, as well as "gurring" cat calls (Figure 28). This behavior constitutes premating

Figure 28 *Rhythmic rolling and "purr" calls tell you that the cat is in heat.*

play, and a cat that is allowed to roam freely will, at about this age, begin its search for a male cat. Should the cat be quite homebound and stay close to the house, as I have observed with at least two cats, they frequently may "receive" male cats from their respective neighborhoods in their yards or patios (male cats instinctively "know" when a female is in heat and ready to mate).

Even male and female cats commonly very affectionate to you will now stop bothering with you. Sometimes they may even react adversely when you approach to stroke and pet them. Right now they are fully occupied with themselves.

It is a little-known fact that cats pick their mates according to their own preferences, and their choices do not reflect the strength and ranking of the tomcats. The latter respect the female's choice in almost all instances. Fights among male cats for ranking appear to impress female cats very little, even though at times they can be observed as spectators.

Mating

Tabby, our half-Angora cat, was in heat and received all the male cats of our neighborhood one warm afternoon on our patio. They all sat in a wide circle, all strong, well-cared-for animals, with the exception of a one-eyed neglected, wild-looking alley cat. This barely grown, slight-of-build, gray-striped lost soul crouched on the sidelines.

Tabby rolled back and forth on the warm patio floor rhythmically, rolling faster and

faster, her long silken coat shining. The male cats' attention was focused exclusively on her. The cat's movements gave the impression of a wild, beautiful dance. Suddenly she came to a dead stop, looked around her as though awakening from a deep sleep, jumped to her feet, fiercely hissed at the male cats, and removed herself by jumping through an open window and settling on the windowsill. From that vantage point she began to call for the slight, small, gray male cat. The many large male cats understood her message quickly and began slowly to beat a retreat.

Only then did the small, gray chosen one draw closer, still hesitant. Tabby continued to call urgently, until he finally climbed over her willingly offered bent back, bit into her neck, and mated with her (even though, in this case, the mating remained without consequences).

Afterwards she did not hiss at him, nor did he receive the often obligatory smack in the face. Tabby just began to slowly retreat.

This smack after mating, which is often accompanied by hissing and is always administered by the female to the male, usually occurs when neither cat knew the other before the pairing and were not familiar with each other.

Females that are familiar with and know a male quite well, and may even have a "friendly relationship" with him, frequently just pretend to go through the motion of smacking or may even avoid it altogether.

The Queen Is Expecting

When your cat returns from the stud male (among purebred cats the female is always taken to the male), she will probably continue to call and roll around, usually until the normal duration of the heat cycle (about 8 days) has elapsed. Within 3–4 weeks you will know with some certainty whether there will be a new litter: the nipples become firmer and rounder and turn a rosy color. Starting in the fifth week, the female will show a definite increase in circumference. During this time the cat's nutritional intake gains special importance, and she should benefit from several small feedings (p. 33). Usually she will begin to search for an appropriate birthing place several weeks before the actual birth, which takes place 62–68 days after successful mating. Her search may include closets, wardrobes, linen closets, and baskets.

You may be successful if you offer a proper birthing place during this stage of her search. It should be placed in a raised area, be free of drafts, preferably be "hidden," and be protected from bright light. A basket, wooden box, or stable carton approximately 15 in. x 25 in. with an edge about 10 in. high is suitable. While the cat should be able to lie comfortably, she should also be able to push against the sides during the actual birth. A firm pillow with a washable cover or a mattress from doll-sized furniture may be used for the bottom cover of the birthing place. Cover the pillow or mattress with a soft, washable cloth or an old blanket, and add thick layers of newspaper and old, soft rags. Wet newspapers and rags may be carefully removed after birth, if the cat tolerates them at all at that point. What you may find practical may not necessarily be agreeable to the animal.

Birth of the Litter

Domesticity and a need for attachment and affection are especially important for most pregnant cats. A properly cared for housecat spends more time than usual at home and with the family, even when she has previously been used to roaming freely.

The first sign of the actual birth is usually the breaking of the water, and with a normal birth labor pains may begin soon after. Many cats, especially when the litter is their first, do not want to be left alone during this phase. They need to know that family members whom they trust are nearby. Our Misty had her first and only litter (of which only one kitten lived and which we were allowed to keep) while we had breakfast—of all times—and demanded to lie between us on the dinette bench. We gave in and quickly made her comfortable in the basket we had previously prepared for her. In quick succession Misty gave birth to two kittens and freed them of their envelopes; then she bit through the umbilical cord and licked them dry (Plate 5). However, suddenly she appeared exhausted and seemed unable to give birth to the last kitten. In a flash it occurred to me to offer her strong coffee with much evaporated milk. She drank greedily, recovered in relatively little time, and gave birth to the third kitten, named Lady, which lived with us for 12 years. By the way, many cats prefer to drink small quantities of liquid, off and on, during the course of giving birth. Therefore it is a good idea to offer watered-down evaporated milk, at body temperature, at regular intervals.

Another cat, a skinny, unwanted animal, also showed a strong need for my presence. I had taken her in and prepared a box for her in a warm corner of our attic near my bedroom. In great despair she repeatedly threw herself against my closed bedroom door, until I relented and took her and her box into my room. She had her litter in front of my bed while I, half asleep, continued to pet her and talk to her in a low voice.

First Days in the Life of a Cat

A newborn kitten is born with all its fur, which is "downlike," softer and warmer than the fur of grown cats. Even the markings are recognizable. The soft ears are tiny and thicker when young, but they are still unable to hear, and the kitten's eyes are closed. As is the case with all newborn mammals, the head is fairly large, the body small, and the musculature still weak. The tiny claws on the paws cannot yet be drawn in.

The first sound of a kitten is a high, thin, piercing scream, not unlike that of an unoiled door. Not much later, on about the third or fourth day, kittens are able to hiss. When we were children, we sometimes passed the time by offering our (strangely scented) fingers to our blind little minitigers, causing them to hiss and make funny faces at us.

At this time the struggle for best place near mother's warm, nursing belly begins. This is amusing to watch because of the kittens' big heads and thin, small bodies.

If you are unable to keep the entire litter, as soon as possible after birth, carefully remove the unwanted kittens with your warm hands, put them in a small, warm basket or carton, and take them to your veterinarian, who will put them to sleep. Depending on the area you live in, sometimes the Humane Society will help. Get as much information as possible before the birth, and perhaps you may need to make an appointment. If you are unable to differentiate between male and female kittens, a veterinarian may have to be consulted. As mentioned above, it is very important to remove the kittens carefully, with warm hands, as well as to wrap and keep them warm; otherwise they are likely to scream and thus alert their mother immediately.

The First Weeks

When just one kitten is left, it is of utmost importance to add some warm rags, such as an old woolen piece of clothing. Usually the members of a litter warm one another. In such cases I have always kept the birthing basket next to my bed in order to quickly cover the chirping, cold little creature when its mother was absent. The mother had free access through the open window.

After barely 1 week the kittens begin to purr for the first time; that happens while they are bedded comfortably next to the mother's belly, and their tongues, shaped like small spoons, are held underneath the nipple. They stimulate the flow of milk by softly kneading their mother's milk sources with their front paws (Figure 29). They know instinctively to do this at the time of their first nursing.

Figure 29 *By clawing and pushing, the kittens stimulate the milk flow of their mother.*

This *milk-kneading* can also be seen among grown cats, occasionally even with their oddly spoon-shaped tongues showing. Satisfied kittens fall asleep in this manner most of the time. This breast kneading always represents an expression of complete contentment, a sense of security—a "memory" of some sort of earthly cat paradise.

During the course of the first week, kittens begin to be able to hear. On about the eighth or ninth day they open their blue eyes; it will take several weeks for their eyes to change to their final color. Their eyes open, not all at once, but slowly, in stages, and as soon as they open completely and shine, the kittens are able to see. Now they begin to follow slowly everything that occurs in their peripheral field of vision. Shortly thereafter they will start to touch or reach for everything that catches their attention. About 3 weeks after birth their first teeth appear, which will be replaced by the permanent dentition starting at about 5 months.

During the first week of life the mother washes (licks) the babies several times every day. She also massages the kitten's belly and anal opening with her tongue in order to assure proper voiding of the excrements, and swallows the contents. While she does this, she stops purring, whereas she continues purring during the rest of the "licking bath." Apparently purring is not compatible with the less attractive duties. Around the 25th day of life kittens usually try to use the litterbox—more or less adeptly, of course.

Some stronger kittens try to resist their mother's cleaning procedures when they are only 3 weeks old. They struggle vehemently to get away; but mother stays consistently strict, without relenting, and, holding the little one with her front paws, works the baby over with her hind paws until the kitten gives in and stops protesting. As soon as the youngsters can sit or stand up, they try to groom themselves. In the beginning they are only slightly coordinated and will lose their balance, toppling over again and again.

Then they start to discover their environment—outside the box, of course—and when they succeed in falling over the edge, they yelp for their mother until she carries them back to safety again. The mother grabs the kitten with her teeth by the scruff of the neck to carry it around. At this time the bite closure is inhibited so that the grip does not hurt the kitten. This grip causes a stiffness (rigor) reflex in the kitten. Carrying a loosely dangling kitten would be not only very hard for the mother, but also dangerous for the kitten. This method is also used when the mother decides to change homes because the first nest is no longer quiet enough or is unsafe, in her opinion. The reflexive stiffness for carrying purposes is the same as that which occurs when the tomcat mates the queen. The stiffening prevents the female from being hurt by the weight of the tomcat or by sudden movements that could injure the spine. The prey animal has the same stiffness reflex; however, the bite closure is not inhibited in this case, so that the cat can actually bite to kill by closing its teeth over the prey.

Transfer of Mothering Behavior

When our Misty raised her kitten Lady, our sons were small children. For weeks Misty reacted not only to the whining of her own kitten but also to the cries of our boys. When one of the boys fell or the other cut his finger, Misty ran quickly to the spot. She checked the area, belligerently growling, and then proceeded to rub her head consolingly against the child.

The Cat Family

My husband and I were included in her motherly care, and from time to time we were presented with the gift of a dead mouse. In Misty's opinion we were just not able to catch our own mice! When she proudly presented the mouse with inviting purring, beckoning for us to take it, I felt quite sorry that we could not accept her generous offer. She maintained this care for us throughout her life, whereas slowly, with time, she lost the mothering behavior toward the boys.

Adopting Other Animal Babies

It is well known that cat mothers are often willing to adopt other animal babies and to feed and raise them. The more frequently occurring species are dogs, the young of rabbits, guinea pigs, and squirrels. However, you must not rely on this behavior, for not all cats are prepared to accept an orphan.

When Cat Mothers Turn into Furies

No matter how shy and fearful the cat, she will turn into a fury when she fears her young to be in danger. Even a large dog that may accidentally walk toward the infants' nest will be attacked without delay or doubt. Before the dog can even assess what has happened, he is turned into a howling, fur-flying bundle of pain on the way to retreat. The animal behaviorist and writer E. S. Thompson tells of a case where a cat mother literally chased a brown bear up a tree in Yellowstone Park!

Cat Games

Young kittens start playing before they can even stand on their little legs. You can be tempted to watch them without noticing that time is flying by, and forgetting all else that needs to be done. They paw their littermates' heads, aim at mother's tail—all clumsily and slowly at first. They run after each other, topple over, or run into the legs of chairs. Coordinated movement needs practice! But they learn very quickly. Kittens at 6 weeks of age already show quite well-balanced motions of remarkable quickness. Endurance, strength, and adeptness have significantly increased. They still tire quickly, though, and they will fall quite suddenly from a wild chase into instant sleep, just as small children do.

Cat mothers that raise only one kitten usually turn quickly young again, and they will act playfully with their only youngster, thus replacing a littermate.

Cat and Mouse

Cat mothers with access to mice will soon catch one for their litters. The kittens will carefully and curiously sniff and nuzzle the dead mouse, not knowing what they are supposed to think or do. The mother cat will then make a deep, growl-like sound, grab the mouse with her teeth, put it down, push it back and forth with her paws, and finally eat it. The kittens, meanwhile, remain observers. Soon thereafter the mother cat will bring a mouse that is only slightly injured. The kittens will chase it, try to touch it, and retreat in terror (Figure 30) when the agonized mouse turns in their direction and possibly bites a kitten's toe or nose. The mother will then proceed to kill the mouse, but the kittens have, by then, started to get the idea. They will lick and

Figure 30   *At first sight of a mouse, the kittens' fear is still strong toward the unknown animal.*

nibble on the leftovers of the mouse. The final lesson takes place when the mother brings a whole, healthy mouse and lets it run before the eyes of the kittens. The mother will stay still and watch, while you can observe how curiosity, fear, and instinctive urge to catch, in turn, get the best of the kittens. Finally, the strongest, most courageous kitten will make the first attack—if it doesn't suffer a bite from the mouse. The little kitten will growl as "fiercely" as it can while it pounces on the mouse. Then the littermates will also approach. When the courageous first hunter realizes the competition, there will be some alarming, deep sounds; and, if these do not prove effective, the kitten will try to get the mouse into a safe place. Pushed by the others, the new hunter will—in desperation—bite strongly enough to kill

the mouse. Thus occur the first successful hunt and a decisive learning experience.

Kittens without littermates usually take longer to learn the same lesson—they frequently just take the mouse from the mother. Mother Misty got quite impatient one day with her only offspring Lady; after repeated escapes of a mouse from Lady's grip, the mother spontaneously smacked her kitten left and right and effectively hard.

"Cat and mouse"—a game of silent approach, sudden jumps, shaking to kill, and carrying around—is also played with balls of string, paper, or anything else, as well as with mother's tail!

Play Fighting

Silent, steathy approaches; sudden jumping attacks, wrangling over and under each other, tails straight up with each hair standing out in a straight line; stiff-legged, sideward and forward lunges . . . all these are typical of kitten play fights, with which they measure their strength and train their agility. Where littermates are missing, the mother adapts easily and joyfully to the needs of the only offspring.

Kitten in a Tree

Every small kitten soon tries to climb—out of the nest box and onto a chair or a sofa, up the drapes—unless you pick it off these places patiently and consistently and engage it otherwise.

We were lucky that our wicker-backed wardrobe survived 15 years of cats climbing

The Cat Family

and sharpening their claws, thus keeping them away from the curtains. A kitten that is allowed to run free outdoors will soon try to climb a tree, led on by its mother, and turns in terror over its own courage—at the top of the tree. There it sits—a small bundle of misery—crying.

I can still see our 3-year-old son Martin under the birch tree where Misty hung, clawed to a top branch: "Now she will never be able to come down again," he sobbed. After a while she did come down after all, unsure, sliding with widely stretched toes and claws. It takes some kittens hours to get enough courage for the descent. If your nerves cannot stand the long tension, you may have to call the Humane Society or the Fire Department (which may or may not respond!). Fortunately, cats learn to climb trees quickly and routinely.

When Kittens Turn into Cats

As long as there is no renewed pregnancy, the ties between mother and kittens remain very close, frequently until at least 3 months. With a single offspring the cat will often tolerate suckling much longer than with multiple offspring, which are weaned by 8–9 weeks, when mother milk is no longer essential. If, however, the cat is pregnant again, she will try to wean her litter even earlier, and she will let her present kittens suckle only as little as necessary and quite unwillingly. If the kittens have reached 8 weeks of age, they are old and strong enough to be weaned. If the kittens are younger than 8 weeks, then you should take great care to feed them adequately.

It is very important for the future wellbeing of cats that their weaning take place slowly over a span of time (pp. 33, 35). This is an important reason why you should not get a kitten younger than 8 weeks old.

If you are dealing with an orphan kitten, you cannot, understandably, insist on establishing an age factor. In such cases the animal simply needs help, and you can raise it into a strong and healthy kitten by providing it with good nutrition, care, and affection. Our orphan Tabby is now a healthy, beautiful, and playful 10-pound cat, despite her arrival in our house at 2 weeks of age as a small, half-starved baby. We attended to her meticulously. While I fed her personally, she was otherwise cared for by our sons in their room. The boys submitted to her increasingly wilder games despite many scratch and bite marks. They loved—and still love—their minitiger, and that tiger loves them back. As far as it may be possible, the boys seemed to have replaced this cat's littermates. Today they are still Tabby's closest reference persons, despite the cat's adult age at present. She shares her favors equally between them by sleeping on the bed of one, and then, when he is watching television, snuggling up to the other with sonorous purring and her inimitable way of batting her eyelids in utter delight.

The Role of the Tomcat in the Cat Family

Tomcats are said to be poor father figures. There seems to be some validity to this saying, as it is true that newborn kittens have occasionally been eaten by their father cats. I have experienced free-roaming cats (e.g., on a farm) where even a passing tomcat was not trusted near the kittens' hiding place; the mother cat would chase any tomcats away—always effectively!

It is quite a different story when a male and a female cat live together in one household. These two animals know each other well, often since their kittenhood, and they will stay close friends through adulthood. In their case one can observe quite different behavior patterns.

When our queen Honey had another litter just 6 months after her first son, Petey, was born, we let her keep, again, a single kitten. Petey was friendly to the new kitten from the first day on. While the mother was out catching mice, he would lie with the baby in its basket and warm it, as soon as the newborn signaled its lonely whining and squirming. As the little "brother" grew older, Petey would play with him, always careful not to hurt him.

One year later the mother cat was pregnant again (Petey was probably the father). The little one had long since found a happy place to live. One morning Petey was watching me working in our greenhouse when the adult female appeared at the door, called, and persisted noisily until the tomboy got up and walked away with her. A little later I looked for them

and found the two in a heap of hay in the shed: one baby was born and already feeding; the next one was on the way. The mother cat looked relaxed and content. The tomcat sat close to her, purring peacefully. As before, we kept only one kitten for the mother; and, as before, Petey warmed and licked the youngster, taking turns with the mother cat. And he didn't tire of playing with the new kitten and keeping it company.

This type of fathering does occur more frequently with tomcats that have been raised with females in the same environment. With neutered males the situation is similar: I knew a neutered male that took warm care of kittens and licked and washed them—he even provided them with mice. This happens not only in homes: I have heard of a tomcat that lived wild and got a spoiled, homebound queen to "elope" with him, never to be seen again. About 4 months later he returned, carrying four kittens, one by one. He let them eat—first—the quickly offered food, and returned them for feeding regularly during the following few weeks. Then they never returned; presumably the kittens had learned to support themselves. Another wilderness tomcat lived in a zoo. When a female had a litter, the tom relinquished his cave hole, brought in food for the mother animal, and gnarled angrily when zoo visitors got too close to the kitten area.

Teaching Tricks to a Cat

Some books on cats give instructions on teaching cats tricks. I am sure that this can

54

be done with patience and friendly persistence, but I don't like the idea.

I find it much more interesting to observe what cats will learn by their own motivation. I find more amusing how cats can train their owners! Lady requested to be let out by standing in front of the door to the garden. She did not consider it necessary to meow. If the door was not immediately opened for her, she would turn her head toward us and give us a look so guilt inducing that one of the family would jump up and oblige her. Lady also wanted to join my husband when he would go for a walk in the evening. She would rub against my husband's legs, take two steps, turn, and wait questioningly. If my husband, in the cat's opinion, slowed down too much, Lady would gently bite the laggard's leg and nudge him in the direction of the garden gate. There she would jump up on the door post, wait to be able to rub her head playfully against my husband's, and balance back and forth over the gate to be petted again and again (Figure 31) until she was satisfied.

Figure 31 *A head rub is a typical ceremony to say hello. The cat expects to be petted.*

Cats are the teachers! When Misty wanted to get in, she would wiggle the keys in the entrance door! I suppose she must have accidentally touched them once—perhaps while she was waiting to be let in, and had stretched her body up along the door—and perhaps just then the door was opened. Since we were easily trained, we opened the door for her from there on each time she "rang." Tabby has a rather weak voice, and she lets us know when she has to get in or out by pounding her front paws against doors, windows, or gates, day or night, effectively enough to make us run to oblige her.

Extraordinary Learning Achievements

Many proud owners are convinced that their cats understand every word they say—not so! Even intelligent cats understand only the intonation, not the word itself. Make the experiment yourself: say to your cat in the usual loving and caressing tone, "You monster! You awful beast!"; your cat will react by purring and rubbing its head against you! But cats do make "discoveries"; they do learn from observation, without experimentation. They not only imitate, but also are capable of spontaneous, considered decisions and actions. Unfortunately, this intelligent behavior is not passed on. This is probably so because the mother-child ties, though intense, are too short in duration, and the general social structure of cats is too loose.

I am going to give you some examples. Misty sat every night on the edge of the bathtub and watched our boys' bath water disappear down the drain. One evening she jumped into the tub just as the last of the water had drained, spread her hindlegs wide over the drain, and voided her urine. She used this drain from then on quite frequently as her "toilet." She had understood the connection. Our friends have a tomcat that actually uses their toilet bowl to go to the bathroom. The bathroom door is left ajar for him. He voids urine silently, but meows when he has a bowel movement!

Our black tom Petey discovered his paws as eating utensils. I used to take the catfood out to the cats in a tall, cylindrical enamel container and from there spoon it out for each cat. Petey must have observed me doing that and found out quickly that his head did not fit in the container. One day I had left some catfood in the enamel pot, and I saw him look at the container and then spoon the food out with his paw, lick it carefully, and continue to eat in this way. Another time I took care of a cat on a farm. That cat had figured out how to open the chicken nest-box flap doors from the inside. She insisted on taking care of her newborn kittens there and agreed to move only when the kittens matured enough to see and walk.

Misty, Lady, and Tabby all catch drops from a dripping faucet and lick their paws when they are thirsty. Tabby, our half-Angora beauty, likes to cool off in the moist bathtub on hot days.

Many cats can open doors. They jump on the handle and press their weight against the door.

Every cat lover can add to my stories from his or her own observations.

Purebred Cats

As with other domesticated animal species, there are numerous breeds of cats. Pure breeds are derived by careful selection of specific standards. They are shown in exhibits and are sold to other cat fanciers. On the contrary, you usually get the ordinary alley or house cats as gifts. They have no breeding standards and are derived from a mixture of parent breeds. But they are just as loving companions, and are just as graceful, as any other cat.

Purebred cats are always recognizable as cats. The differences in the external appearance of a particular breed are less variable than with alley cats, though. I personally consider the tailless Manx cat and the wavy-haired Rex cat a bit far out. In this chapter I shall discuss only the most commonly known types of purebred cats.

European Short-Hair Cat

These felines are most similar in body structure to the domesticated tabby wildcat, and they are bred in many strictly fixed color combinations (Figure 32). They may

Figure 32 *Two common house cat types: left, the plump, squat type; right, the slender type.*

have any eye color to be found in cats. This breed is known to be friendly, playful, and undemanding (Plate 6).

Siamese Cat

This cat probably originates from Bengalese felines in Southeast Asia. These animals are slim, lithe, and muscular, and they have a narrow, wedge-shaped head; long, slender legs; and a long, thin tail. Their base color is ivory with contrasting dark markings that give the face a masklike look and occur also on ears, paws, or tail (Figure 33). The eyes are blue. Kittens are light colored, with the dark markings developing only with time.

Figure 33 *A Siamese cat: the basic coat color is cream; the eyes are deep blue.*

Siamese cats are quite temperamental and noisy. The mating calls of unneutered animals are bound to annoy neighbors. Siamese cats need—more than others—close contact with their human reference person. They also need more attention, toys, and opportunities for play, and they tolerate being left alone less well, than do other cats (Plate 4).

Cats

Abyssinian Cat

These cats are of light weight and elegant build and remind one of old Egyptian cat sculptures. The short, thick haircoat was originally hare-colored, and the eyes are green-yellow or topaz. Today you can find this breed with red, blue, silver, cream, and lavender hair coats. Abyssinians are said to be actively playful and closely attached to their owners (Plate 4).

Havannah Cat

These cats are slim and agile and have elegant proportions. The tail is long; the hindlegs are a little longer than the forelegs. The coat is short, dense, and shiny, and the color is a smooth, even brown of varying tones. The eyes are green.

Rex Cat

The Rex is of medium height, muscular, and sleek, and has long, slender legs. The dense and velour-like coat is like that of the Rex rabbit, slightly curly and wavy, especially along the back and tail. Even the whiskers and eyebrows are curly. Occasionally, Rex cats produce nude or partially hairless kittens. I hope that this accident will not be used to develop a new cat breed! It would probably result in a distortion with ill health. This special breed did not develop until 1950 and then by way of a spontaneous mutation—of course, it happened in England, the land of cat breeders!

Persian Cat

Persian cats used to be called "Angora cats," a name that was eliminated in 1965. The long-hair Pallas' cat of Central Asia is believed to be the ancestor of the domestic Persian cat. By selective methods, using long-hair offspring, these cats were developed in England to their present standards. There they are now called "long-hair cats." Persians are rather heavy but not clumsy. The head must be large and round, with a broad forehead; widely set, small ears; a broad, short nose; round cheeks; and large eyes. The face is framed by a fine furry collar, and the tail is short and fluffy. Many coat colors are available now, and all colors of eyes can also be seen (Figure 34). Persian cats are quieter in nature, loving, and friendly. They are thus very suitable as indoor cats. They are also the most willing to walk on leash and harness.

Figure 34 *Persian cats come in different coat and eye colors.*

They cannot, however, manage their own long fur coats. These cats must be combed and brushed; otherwise their hair will

Purebred Cats

become matted and they will swallow too much hair while grooming. Most white Persian cats with blue eyes are deaf. To these Persian breeds also belongs the famous Colorpoint cat (see also Plate 3 and back cover).

Colorpoint–Long-Hair Cat

This cat was once called the Khmer cat. It has a light-colored body with dark markings, showing the same color variations as does the Siamese cat. The Colorpoint cat was bred originally, about 50 years ago, in France and Germany. Although this cat may resemble a Birman cat (see below), it never shows their characteristic white feet. These animals are beautiful but are of slow temperament. Once adult, they seek much sleep, love to be caressed, and rarely show interest in play. These may just be the characteristics that make them the choice of some cat fancier.

Birman Cat

This cat has a body equally long and solid and stands on short, strong legs. The long, silky fur is slightly curly on the belly, and the tail is fluffy like a feather brush. White feet are the color characteristic (Figure 35). The fur colors are the same as those of the short-hair Siamese cat, so you can find them as Seal-pointed (i.e., with brownish markings) or as Blue-pointed (i.e., with bluish markings). The eyes must always be deep blue. A legend tells of the development of the sacred temple cats,

Figure 35 *Characteristics of the Birman cat: fluffy tail, neck mane, white paws.*

which is another name for Birmans. According to the legend, these cats were close companions for Mediterranean priests. The true derivation of the Birman cat is not definitively established.

Turkish Cat

The Turkish or Van Cat has half-long, silky hair, and originates around Van Lake in eastern Turkey. This cat is as sturdy and resistant as a mixed-breed house cat, and it is said to resent water less than other cats do.

The long, yet squat body is supported by medium-long legs. There are fluffy hair brushes on the delicate toes; the tail is medium long, fluffy, and chestnut colored with pale rings, while the body fur is chalk white. Chestnut markings outline the delicate, widely set ears. Rosy colored are the nose, foot pads, and skin. The large, round eyes are the color of amber.

This breed was first purebred in England after an English woman introduced the cats to Britain in 1955.

Understanding Cats: A Special Chapter

Ancestors of the Domestic Cat

Considering all we know today, we believe that the African tabby wildcat was the sleek, agile ancestor of our domesticated house cat. Those ancestor cats were valued in old Egypt as easily tamed home companions, and they were then already cherished and venerated in temples. They were considered sacred animals of the goddess Bast, in whose temples they became welcome small substitutes for the lions previously used.

The Greeks acquired cats from the Egyptians, and trade brought the animals to Rome. Phoenicians carried cats with them at sea and probably brought them to Britain. The domesticated cats mated freely with the European wildcats, which are today an endangered species. You can see various cat types in special zoos if you have the patience and interest to track them to their usual hiding places.

Two major types of domestic cats developed from these crossbreeds: the tabby cat, the slender type, with relatively long legs, a delicate narrow head, and slim tail; and the wildcat, or more plump or squat type, which is short-legged and sturdy, with a rounded, broader head and a shorter, fluffier tail without an actual point. The underhair of the wildcat is denser than that of the tabby cat. The pure breeds (the aristocrats) supposedly developed from crosses of the tabby and other smaller cats from various countries. There also occurred a number of mutations during the process of domestication, which changed color, fur, and body structure. These changes, however, were much less marked than in the development of dogs.

The Nubian Tabby Cat

These small, slender cats have a small head, large ears, and a long pointed tail. Their basic fur color is yellowish gray to yellowish brown, with variable markings, flecked, or striped, or without any markings, along back and sides. The back is significantly darker, but shows no median mark line. Wild tabbies live in grass and bushlands of Africa and Arabia, never in rain forests or sand deserts.

The European Wildcat

Since domestic cats, which derived from the wild tabby cats, were introduced, the major breeds have often crossbred. Even today, the tabby-wildcat type is still frequently seen. You may remember a well-publicized incident in Germany where a "true wild tabby cat" was found in a wooded area close to a city. Since wildcats there were a protected species, this animal was caught and taken into protective care for supplemental feeding. The case was publicized, and soon an owner came to the cat shelter, where he was greeted very affectionately by his "wild" cat—which was willingly taken home. There you have an example of how similar wildcats and domestic cats can still be.

The European wildcat has only a few survivors in small areas of Middle Europe, where such cats were considered a dangerous menace and most were eradicated long ago. During the adaptation of the European wildcats to the Middle-European climate (cool weather and forests), these animals grew larger and sturdier, with shorter ears and tails than the original tabby cats. Also, a plusher, softer fur developed, especially in winter, when the undercoat became extra long and dense. The original yellowish gray color often turns silvery during winter, and the horizontal lines become paler. The only remaining significant and unchanged markings are the facial marking, four longitudinal lines across the neck, the narrow blackish ridge along the back, the dark rings around calves and tail, and the black tip of the tail (Figure 36). Even

Figure 36 *Portrait of a European wildcat. The teeth are stronger, and whiskers are longer, than those of the house cat.*

wildcats prefer sunny and warm places, and despite their good thermal protection they usually live in milder climates or forests. They love sunbathing just as much as do our house cats.

During the summer months these cats prefer the edge of a forest or wooded fields where adjoining grass and grain fields offer a plentitude of prey. Their main hunt for food is aimed at mice, but they also catch birds occasionally—usually young or sick animals—as well as young hares, wild young rabbits, and some large beetles and crickets. Only a few animals will catch fish, which they can do extremely well with their agile, quick paws. During the winter months they prefer mixed forests, especially south and southeast zones. Heavily snowbound areas are dangerous for cats. They are too heavy, and their feet are too small to prevent them from sinking into the snow. Also, mice just aren't caught easily underneath a layer of snow!

Most wildcats live singly. However, during the summer the male cats are friendly with all females. Females try to chase away any males entering their territory, except during their mating cycles.

Courting and mating take place between February and March. Two to four offspring are born after a gestation of 68 days. These kittens are just as helpless as those of house cats, and their development takes the same course. The mother cat selects a dry, protected place, close to abundant prey, long before the delivery time. She cares for her offspring with the same attachment and care as domesticated breeds do.

When the young are about 3 months old, the mother cat chases them away from her territory to fend for themselves. She needs her own territory to build up enough body weight for winter. Young wildcats are mature at 1 year of age, but their growth is not complete until they are about 2 years old. The life span of both wildcats and domestic cats is about 12–15 years.

Cats

The Social Life of Domestic Cats

You have now learned much about the relationship of queen and tom in a cat family, about families with or without a father, about raising a cat, and about cat games. Yet there is more for you to know in order to be able to understand your cat as fully as possible.

"The Home of First Order"
Animal behaviorists call "the home of first order" the place where the cat actually lives. This is not a great deal. It usually consists of the living area in the house, the persons who are close to the animal, and in rural areas also a shed or barn. This home always offers one or, more likely, several rest places that are safe, quiet, and comfortable. Usually it is lived in alone or with a few close cat friends. Friends are usually tolerated only when each has enough territory to get away from the others when the mood requires solitude.

The human companions are willingly tolerated as a sort of supercats, rather than as part of the environment.

Significantly, cats usually act quite naturally and self-assuredly in their homes. My husband once mentioned the feeling that he was just renting the place from the cats!

Even in the home of first order a hierarchy will be established. Usually the cat of highest rank will get the best sleeping place. This place may be taken by another cat only when it is vacated. The higher ranking cat will rarely chase the lower ranking cat from the preferred place; however, quite frequently, the lower animal

will voluntarily give up the spot. I have also observed, though, that the No. 1 cat will join No. 2 in the basket and start stretching until No. 2 is squeezed right out of the desirable spot.

My very dear, "cat-fanatic" relatives keep seven queens and toms in a medium-sized apartment, which, however, adjoins a vast parkland. It works well for them because all animals have their own specific places, which all others respect. Even the hat rack is taken! There are rarely any scenes around the well-stocked feeding place, because the cats don't all eat at the same time.

There are also cat households where cats live with each other without any differences in rank and behave like equal friends. They lie with each other, warm and groom each other, and play together throughout adulthood. This will occur more frequently when there are not more than two animals in a household. Many cats are distinctly defensive of their homes against strange cats or dogs and unfamiliar persons. This behavior may be apparent against a holiday cat sitter with whom the cat was not familiar!

The Territory
The territory that surrounds the "home of first order" and consists of a back or front yard, gardens, and maybe a meadow or field will not usually be defended by your cats. At most, they may chase away strange animals, but neighbor cats are usually tolerated: they have the "right to pass," although actual face-to-face contacts are avoided. When they do meet, both cats will stand still until one decides to move on

64

slowly, while the other waits courteously until the distance has grown sufficiently between them.

Tomcat Fights

The rank order of four cats in adjoining territories is decided by fighting (Figure 37). Weaker animals, however, stay the

Figure 37 *Tomcats fight to establish orders of rank and decide over queens.*

No. 1 animal in their own territories. When neighboring toms meet inadvertently, the rule is that the lower animal may pass peacefully unless it insists on crossing the higher ranking tom's path too closely. The hierarchial order among cats is not as strict as in many other species. Tomcats in one general area usually defend that community territory together against strange intruders.

Only young toms, up to about 1 year of age, have a fool's freedom—and even in their first combats, they are treated with softer paws than are adult toms. The older toms entice the young ones to fight with almost tender sounds. During the second year of life, however, things turn serious

for the newcomers, and they have to withstand many tough fights. As Professor Leyhausen tells, it often takes shredded ears, torn noses, and many bite wounds before the young tom is accepted into the "fraternity" of mature male cats.

Should a youngster try to get involved in the fight between "macho males," they will just chase him away, not by attacking but only by threatening. Cat children should stay away from these serious fights! I had a chance to observe this myself: my black tom Petey had a fight with one of his neighbors while their mutual favorite queen sat watching on a windowsill. There advanced slowly and silently one of the 6-month-old kittens from next door. At sight of him the adults stopped their fight immediately, and both went about threatening the curious youngster into fearful retreat.

With a true tom fight goes a true battle song: repeated chords of high-pitched meowing, howling, and deep growling. During the battle the attacker tries to bite the opponent in the neck, upon which the latter falls on his back to free all four sharp-clawed paws, plus his fierce teeth. Then the two will tumble, entwined, on the floor with loud screams, separate, threaten each other, and start all over. This goes on until one decides to sit down and refuses to continue. Usually the winner will then no longer attack, nor will he pursue the loser when the latter slinks away. This may be so, in part, because his muscles are still too tensed for him to run after the escapee.

The Cat's Anatomy

Teeth

Feline dentition is especially developed for carnivorous (meat-eating) nutrition. In each half of the jaw—the upper as well as the lower—there are three small incisors and one strong, saber-shaped canine tooth. Next to this tooth you will observe a space, which is followed by three upper and two lower premolars and one molar each. The upper molar is quite small. To bite off a piece of material the cat does not use the incisors, as we human beings do; rather, cats use the upper last premolar and the lower strong molar. The front teeth are used to nibble small pieces of meat off a bone with the help of the rough tongue.

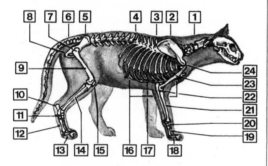

Figure 38   *Anatomy of the domestic cat.*

1. Vertebrae of the neck. 2. Shoulder blade.
3. Chest vertebrae. 4. Back vertebrae.
5. Lower-back vertebrae. 6. Tail vertebra.
7. Pelvic joint. 8. Pelvis. 9. Femur. 10. Heel.
11. Tarsal bones. 12. Metatarsal bones. 13. Toes.
14. Tibia, shin. 15. Patella. 16. Chest plate.
17. Chest, thorax. 18. Toes. 19. Metatarsal
bones. 20. Wrist. 21. Radius, ulna.
22. Elbow joint. 23. Humerus.
24. Shoulder joint.

Velvet Paws

All cats walk on their toes. The strongly developed foot pads (there are well-developed sweat glands between them) serve to allow equilibrium body weight on all the foot pads, which, in turn, allows the cats their silent movements. Don't presume, however, that cats are always silent! When they are unobserved and feel quite sure of themselves, they can behave clumsily and noisily. I have often been angry when, while I wanted to sleep, my cats chose to race and stomp about.

All cats have five toes on their front feet. The "thumbs," however, are very short, and they do not touch the ground. There are four toes on the hind paws. The first toe is present only as a rudimentary small stump. Hair grows between toes and foot pads, but there is no hair at all on the surface of the foot pads.

Sharp Claws

The curved sharp and pointed claws of cats are their most reliable weapon. Normally the claws are pulled inside the skin pockets provided, and are extended only for specific uses such as defense, climbing, hunting, and sharpening. Newborn kittens cannot yet control their claws. They cannot pull them back until they are several days old.

The Senses—Seeing, Hearing, Smelling, and Feeling

Vision

Domestic cats have about the same daylight vision as human beings. Their sensitivity to light, though, especially short-wave illumination, is about six times as great.

Cat eyes can very quickly adapt to darkness. Light, even of very low intensity, can be reflected and used because of the structure of cats' eyes (Figure 39).

Figure 39 *Cat eyes: the pupils are open in the dark but become narrow slits in the light.*

Hearing

Cats have excellent hearing, which enables them to detect very faint noises that human beings cannot hear. They can also accurately place the source of a minute sound (e.g., the movement of mice underground), a capacity that serves them well when they are hunting for rodents.

The external ear shell is quickly (as the initially perceived sound requires) turned in the assessed direction and thus functions like a sound-funnel amplifier. Cat hearing is optimal between 500 hertz and 7 kilohertz. At frequencies higher than 12 kilohertz human hearing is better than that of cats.

Smelling

The olfactory sense of cats is also excellently developed. Cats can recognize the typical odor of familiar animals and distinguish the smell of new cats in the territory. When cats identify the odor of a strange cat, they immediately become more alert and careful. Professor Paul Leyhausen, a well-known behaviorist, believes that cats then inform their fellows in the territory by spraying urine very finely along territorial borders or other places. Thus, he postulates, a cat comes along and smells a fresh urine "mark," which signals "Stop—careful"; if the mark is no longer fresh, it signals "Proceed with care" ; and if the mark is old, it means "Go ahead—the territory is clear!" Hunting territories usually overlap. Cats prefer to go hunting singly, and for this purpose the time-indicative odor marking is very practical and effective, and avoids head-on collisions.

Feeling

The whiskers over the mouth, as well as those over the eyes and inside the front feet, are longer and stronger than the body hair. There are hair follicle receptors (nerves at the roots of the hairs) in these areas, which allow the whiskers to bend and narrow their direction for a specific opening or hole. Without these sensory hairs, cats would be quite insecure, especially in darkness. They need the sensory hairs to assess narrow passages.

Equilibrium Reflexes

House cats, like their wild ancestors, climb high and therefore need a well-developed equilibrium for survival. Changes in the equilibrium release reflexive changes in body positioning, which in turn enable cats to free-fall from a height of about 15 feet onto the ground. Their long axis turns from the back to the ventral position, and they land on their feet. In so doing, the head turns first, followed by the torso and then by the hindlegs, to regain the normal position (Plate 2).

The sensory hairs are also important for the perception of space and for equilibrium.

Cat Language

Cats can express quite clearly exactly what they feel. Social contacts are of greater importance in a cat's life than is commonly assumed. These include the closest and most intense ties between mother and kitten; the informal friendship between adult animals; relationships at the time of mating, and during nightly get-togethers, which might be described as "cozy visits with appropriate distance"; and also the close ties with "their" persons. All of the above ties can, quite obviously, be differentiated only because of a multitude of options in communication.

Body Language
A relaxed body posture can be considered equivalent to a relaxed voice. This is achieved only when the animal feels well and safe. This condition is then expressed in posture, walk, sitting position, and resting position. Relaxation and mental peace are also expressed by engagement in thorough grooming (Figure 40). Nervous or disquieted animals will show—at the most—sporadic grooming gestures that show obvious lack of concentration. When cats

Figure 40 *A cat washes itself: a sign of relaxation and undisturbed condition.*

are completely relaxed, they will have their eyes half or completely shut while they sit or lie. At least the pupils will be narrowed to a slit. The desire to rest, doze, or sleep is expressed by various relaxed resting positions, such as curled up or stretched out long, on one side or in the "classic" way with paws folded under the chest (we call this "muffy" because the front paws look like a muff, in this position). Cats, like human beings, dream only during deep sleep, not while dozing or sleeping lightly. Sometimes you can imagine what they are dreaming when you watch their movements, for example, their paws, mouths, and whiskers. After a nap you can observe the cat stretching into an intense hunchback, then stretching long with a yawn—these are signs of comfort and inner peace. A cat awakes slowly.

Head rubbing is the tender greeting ceremony between friendly cats, mothers and kittens, cats and "their" owners. Not only the head but also the body and flanks are affectionately rubbed against the individual greeted. Along with this greeting behavior goes a tail carried straight up in the air—a sign of a happy, relaxed mood (Figure 41). When cats nuzzle each other when they meet, this indicates just as much affection as it looks like—very similar to a kiss!

Figure 42 *Alert observation: tense body posture, with ears turned toward the front.*

Figure 41 *In this posture, which is often accompanied by purring, the cat greets the close person.*

Alertness is the case when you see the body tense and the ears forward, listening (Figure 42). If, however, the ears are laid flat back, the muscles are tense, the fur is slightly ruffled, and the tail is moving heavily—then you are looking at a cat ready to attack and fight. It will mean ready defense if a paw is lifted additionally. Intense fright produces a tensed body, flattened ears, and low ducking along the floor (Figure 43). It is obvious that fear and aggressiveness have similar behavioral patterns, one emotion being latent in the

other, just as a person is both angry and fearful when pushed into a tight spot. Therefore, if you cannot avoid placing your cat in a frightening situation (e.g., during a visit to the veterinarian), be understanding and careful. When a cat panics, it may become desperately aggressive. One of my most docile cats tore herself suddenly from me once while I held her on the veterinarian's table for an injection of

Figure 43 *Aggressive position: lowered body with silent approach and intense concentration just before the jump.*

Cats

anesthetic. She pounced at me, landing a large, bloody scratch across my cheek, and then hid under the table. I felt truly sorry for her, since she would not have had to act so desperately without this unusual circumstance. Fear is characterized in a cat by the hair standing up on end; the tail looks like a bottle brush, and the hairs along the back are straight up like a long comb (Figure 44). The entire animal looks

Figure 44 *Defense reaction: fear—threatening, with hissing and hair coat standing up.*

larger that way, thus impressing the opponent. The threatening behavior is further heightened by arching the back high, curling the nose, pulling the corners of the mouth way back, and turning the ears outside. In this fashion mother cats will typically frighten away dogs that come too close to their kittens. They do not pounce forward, but rather approach with fierce determination sideways, presenting the long side of their bodies—again, I assume, to appear larger.

The same type of galloping threat movements can be observed in young and older cats for the mere sake of play-fighting. When our Tabby is out in the yard and we walk out at night, she will frequently play-attack us in that fashion, and when we clumsily reciprocate she will exaggerate her battle threats in most comic ways.

Most dog owners quickly identify a wagging tail motion as a friendly gesture. But the beating of a cat's tail from side to side has a quite different meaning and characterizes high tension and excitement. The faster and heavier the tail beats, the stronger is the nervous excitement. You can observe this behavior before fights and during the slow approach toward the pounce on a prey animal, as well as when the cat is playing with the prey.

Sound Language

"Meow" is the characteristic sound of cat language, but it comes in many different, expressive tonalities: imploring, demanding, questioning, excited, and sad. With some practice you will soon understand which meaning is expressed. The mating tomcat sounds a version with a rolling "r"—and as children we quickly found translations for their "words!"

A "gurring," deep "rr," ending in a higher tone, is always meant to sound tender. That is how mother cats talk to their babies, kittens to their mothers, and toms to their chosen queens; also, queens make that sound during their heat cycle. All tame, friendly cats talk like that to "their" owners.

Purring expresses comfort and a feeling of safety. Can you imagine anything more peaceful than a purring cat in a room? Kittens purr while they suckle on their mother; cat mothers purr when they feed and lick their babies. Every cat purrs when

Understanding Cats: A Special Chapter

Figure 45 *The domestic cat as an example for behavioral studies.*
Row 1 (from top to bottom): a) Quiet, well balanced b) Alert c) Concentrated, observant
Row 2 (from top to bottom): a) Disquieted b) Threatening c) Threat-growling
Row 3 (from top to bottom): a) Threat-howling b) Threat-hissing c) Screaming and attacking

a comfortable pillow invites it for a nap. The loudness of the sounds varies among individuals.

A chattering treble is sounded for urges, especially when the prey is far away: birds, butterflies, flies, and beetles at a distance or behind the window.

Hissing, with curled nose and distorted face, expresses undeniably and definitely animosity.

Gnarling expresses both a warning for the opponent, and instructions to kittens about impending danger. Gnarling will be heard when a dog barks or a disliked person passes. The kittens understand the voice and are cautious—which may occasionally save their lives. Repeatedly one can observe that kittens are less fearful—thus more endangered—if they were removed too early from their mothers. A phase of childhood education is noticeably missing here.

Long-drawn-out howling in low and high wavering tones, with a brief, sudden, final hissing, is the usual prelude of tomcats for battle. It reminds me of the ancient Greek custom where war heroes went into long tirades of mutual abuse before battles.

Cats with Behavioral Disturbances

A strong experience of fear and physical or emotional deficiencies can lead to disturbances of cat behavior. Also, an excessively restricted territory of little space and a lack of activities can produce such disturbances, when physical exercise and natural instinct cannot be used to fulfill innate urges to play.

This situation is not always the owner's fault. Misty was ready for another mating while Lady was still a very small kitten, and soon another litter was on the way. When Lady was only 6 weeks old, her mother started to be rough with her; and when the kitten wanted to suckle, the mother often pushed her quickly away and walked off. Misty cleaned her only rarely and then inattentively. More and more frequently Misty hissed at the kitten when she rubbed her mother's body, wanted warmth, or asked to play. The natural process of weaning was accelerated and shortened because the mother cat was trying to save her strength for her new litter.

We could not fully replace this lack of mothering for Lady, despite the fact that we fed her well and gave her all kinds of attention and love. As soon as the mother cat was around, Lady acted frightened, yet she always wanted to drink from Misty. I wanted Lady to profit from mother's milk as long as possible, and so had Misty sterilized only a short time before the delivery, thereby killing the kittens since I could not have placed them.

Two days after surgery, when Misty was well back on her legs, she started to treat Lady like a newborn baby. Even though she was well into kitten infancy by then, Misty was frantic when she left the basket and jumped around happily, while the mother sat in her basket calling and gnarling in great concern. If nothing else worked, Misty would jump after the big baby, grab her by the scruff of the neck, and drag her back into the "litter's" nest. This was especially difficult because Lady had passed the age of falling into the typical carrying stiffness, but rather scrambled about while she was being dragged. Mother was happy only when the infant was close to her and suckling. Lady wanted to know nothing of being washed, cleaned, or "diapered." Misty was completely geared for a newborn litter, and she found herself pushed into substituting her prior offspring, Lady, for the litter that had been taken away. Consequently, Lady

Understanding Cats: A Special Chapter

was confused because of insecurity, and fearful and aggressive at the same time. This is similarly found in human behavior!

Lady was moody with strangers as well as with us. Sometimes a petting hand was suddenly smacked, or a warning, unwilling sound was followed by a quick bite. These behavior patterns are uncommon for healthy, normal cats.

I received our tomcat Butch, an orphan, in a state of extreme fear and blind terror. He was brought to us in a tin bucket with a perforated lid, dangling from the handlebars of a motorcycle—after a 2-hour ride! The cause of this incredible transport was not cruelty or negligence; it was pure ignorance!

The poor little fellow spent the first few days in our house under a large cupboard—his eyes wide open—eating only when nobody was around. I tiptoed around him and tried to whisper, for the most part, to him, since noise was a main cause of his disturbed behavior. With time he became more trusting, tolerated my caresses, and got used to normal voices without fear. Finally his equilibrium was restored sufficiently so that he could be let outdoors. He discovered and "conquered" the garden slowly, and turned into a free-running tomcat with all the normal activities of catching mice and fighting for love and play. However, he never lost a panic fear of motor noises!

Tabby had been found by our children in the field where the cat lay half-starved with three newborn kittens. She has still not overcome her hunger fixation: in quite unfeline manner she devours her food with the speed of light, despite our regular and

sufficient meal supplies. When she did this initially, she would frequently regurgitate the quickly eaten food. Therefore I changed her food to finely ground meat, which consequently stayed down even after her hasty eating. In order to get her to chew and to give her teeth and gums proper action, I started her on cat biscuits, and—sure enough—she began nibbling and cracking! She seems to tolerate her hasty swallowing when it comes to milk and soft foods, for she still does it today.

These examples have, I hope, shown you that neuroses can develop also in animals after bad experiences.

A cat can develop normally and stay that way only when it is kept and cared for properly, with consideration for its specific characteristics and needs.

"False" Cats—Do They Exist?

An old aunt of ours, who did not like cats at all, once asked how we could possibly live with these "false animals." My husband answered: "How so? We have only genuine cats!"

Joking aside, cats show their feelings, and they warn you of impending aggression or defense in unmistakable ways. From some experiences, though, I must conclude that exceptions may well exist. Here is an example. Mitzi was an orphan when I started caring for her. She expressed her appreciation by extra-close attachment to me. Then we acquired a shepherd dog, Senta, a poor fearful animal that had been passed from owner to owner several times. In order to avoid any head-on collisions, I

took Mitzi in my arms and held Senta at
her neckband, while I talked to both of
them about how they should get along
together and neither was to hurt the other.
I am sure they didn't know a word I had
said, but they both understood my message.
The dog was calm; the cat was not
frightened.

Then an occurrence took place that was
repeated evening after evening identically:
Senta would lie in the grass behind the
house; the cat approached, purred tenderly,
rubbed her head lovingly against the
dog—all perfectly normal cat greetings—but
then, suddenly and incredibly fast, she
would smack the dog's ears with her sharp
claws and run away. Senta, a very docile
dog, did not even dare to pursue or
threaten her. The dog just stood there
miserably with her tail between her
hindlegs—a pitiable picture to watch! I do
not know what could have been the cat's
reasons. However, looking at her sitting at
a distance, she suggested quite human
interpretations.

Also, dogs are known to behave this
way—and that proves their intelligence
more than it could prove falseness. And
yet, nobody talks about "false" dogs. There
exists an unreasoning, widespread prejudice
against cats. I hope that this prejudice will
eventually disappear and that this book will
contribute to that end.

Books to Enhance Your Knowledge and Understanding of Cats

1. *The Well Cat Book: The Cat Lover's Illustrated Medical Compendium*
T. McGinnis, D.V.M.: Random House—Bookworks, New York.

2. *My Cat's in Love, or How to Survive Your Feline's Sex Life, Pregnancy, Kittening*
Frank Manolson, D.V.M.: St. Martin's Press, New York.

3. *The Everlasting Cat*
Mildred Kirk: The Overlook Press.

4. *The Silent Miaow: A Manual for Kittens, Strays, and Homeless Cats*
Paul Gallico: Crown Publishers, New York.

5. *The Natural Cat: A Holistic Guide for Finnicky Cat Owners*
Anitra Frazier: Putnam-Harbor, New York.

6. *What Your Cat Is Trying to Tell You*
Carol C. Wilbourn, Cat Therapist: Macmillan Publishing Company, New York.

7. *The Complete Cat Encyclopedia*
Grace Pond, Ed.: Crown Publishers, New York.

German Publications Referred to in Text
1. *Verhaltensstudien an Katzen* (*Studies on Cat Behavior*)
Paul Leyhausen: Parey Verlag, Berlin.
2. *Rassekatzen* (*Purebred Cats*)
Rosemarie Wolff and Helga Braemer: Belser Verlag, Stuttgart.

- The book list supplies an abundance of detailed information on all aspects of cat care, purchase, and breeding.
- Animal shelters are listed in the telephone books for cities and counties.
- Breeders of purebred and mixed-breed cats are listed in the telephone book; local, state, and national newspapers; pet magazines; and pet shops.
- Cat fancier associations and federations are also listed in cat encyclopedias.

Index

Italic type indicates the location of color photographs.

Index

Index